D1456326

THIS IS ANTARCTICA

Here is an exciting report on that strange but beautiful continent at the bottom of the earth — Antarctica — where man has eked out a way of life through heroism, determination and hope, in spite of danger and hardships.

In this fascinating account, Joseph Dukert explores all aspects of life on the frozen continent including its early history, the treacherous and often tragic expeditions to conquer it, the animal life and natural wonders found there. He introduces us to the modern Antarctican, describing how he lives, works and travels, enduring the terrible climate and bare necessities of life with humor and enthusiasm.

Most important, he discusses the scientific explorations and discoveries now going on. These scientific missions shape tomorrow's hopes and eventually will make them possible through the icebreakers, airplanes and atomic power which are revolutionizing life in Antarctica.

THIS IS ANTARCTICA

Illustrated with photographs and drawings by John T. Gorsuch

THIS IS

ANTARCTICA

by Joseph M. Dukert

Coward-McCann   New York

ACKNOWLEDGMENTS

Grateful acknowledgment is made for permission to use the following:

Photograph on page 181 from Alpine Geophysical Associates

Photograph on pages 94-95 from the Australian News and Information Bureau, Norosti Press Agency

Photograph on page 179 from the Australian Press and Information Division

Photograph on page 29 by Joseph Dukert

Photograph on page 114, Lockheed Photo

Photographs on title page and pages 15, 52, 106, 123, 133, 140, 146-147, 148, 149, 151, 153, 154, 157, 183 from the Martin Company

Photograph on page 49 from National Archives

Photographs on jacket and pages 32, 41, 57, 61, 62, 67, 71, 80, 91, 122, 137, 164, 169, 174 from the National Science Foundation

Photograph on page 44 from the Norsk Folkesmuseum, Oslo

Photograph on page 77, Norwegian Official Photo

Photographs on pages 12-13, 16, 17, 18, 24-25, 27, 28, 31, 35, 43, 50, 53, 54, 55, 65, 78, 79, 82, 85, 86, 88, 89, 93, 111, 112, 120, 126, 129, 130, 135, 139, 141, 142, 143, 144, 155, 162, 167, 171, 185, from the U. S. Navy

© 1965 by Coward-McCann, Inc.

Library of Congress catalog Card Number: 65-20379

MANUFACTURED IN THE UNITED STATES OF AMERICA
102015

To Ginny

CONTENTS

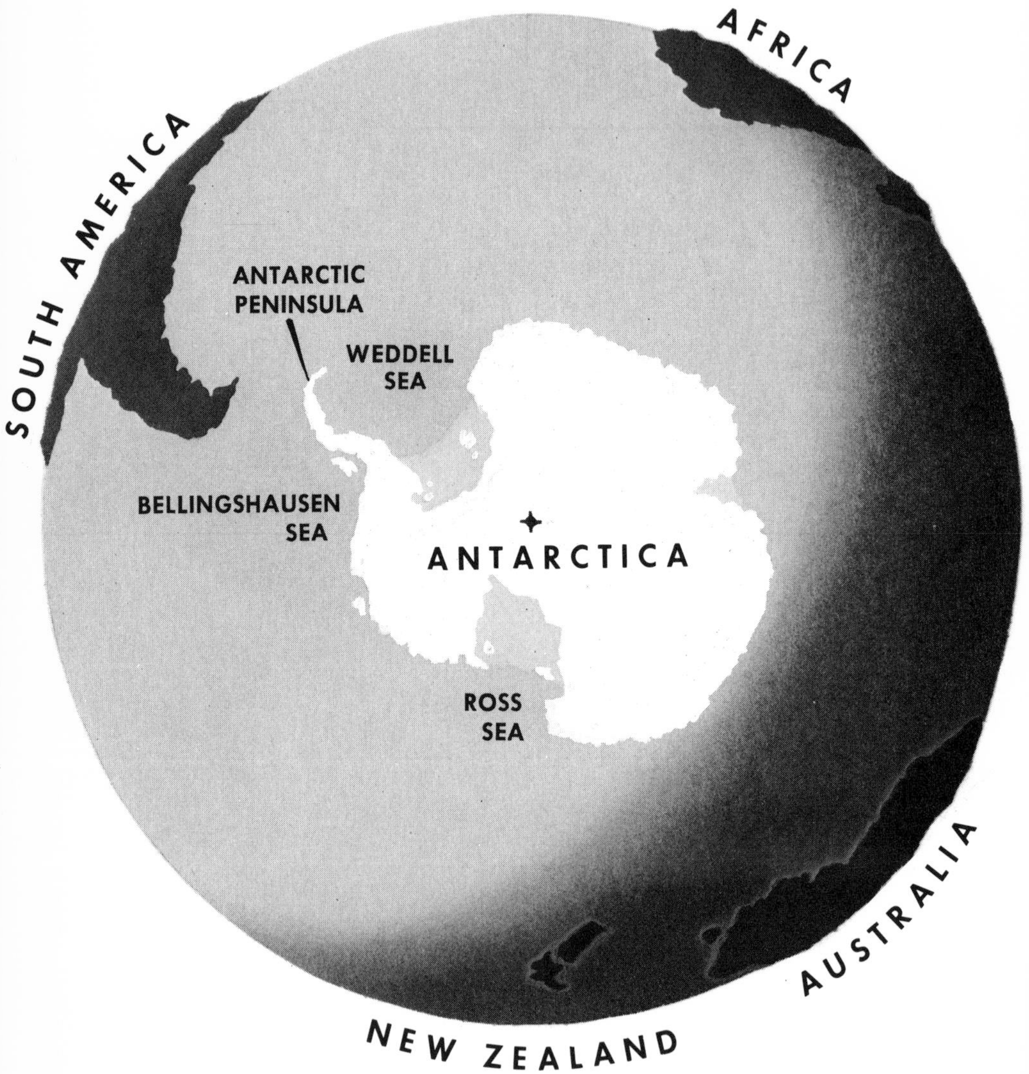

AFRICA

SOUTH AMERICA

ANTARCTIC
PENINSULA

WEDDELL
SEA

BELLINGSHAUSEN
SEA

ANTARCTICA

ROSS
SEA

AUSTRALIA

NEW ZEALAND

THIS IS ANTARCTICA

CHAPTER ONE

Introduction to the Unknown

Imagine a place as big as the United States and Europe combined. Sunnier than California, yet colder than the freezing compartment of your refrigerator. Drier than Arabia and higher than mountainous Switzerland. Emptier than the Sahara desert. Only one place in the world fits the description. It is Antarctica, the strange but beautiful continent at the bottom of the earth.

12

This view of Cape Hallett is typical
of Antarctica's dreamlike beauty.

Antarctica's recorded history is brief. Only a few thousand men have ever set foot on the continent, and many parts of it remain uncharted. In fact, very little of its ground surface will ever be seen . . . because Antarctica is covered by more than nine-tenths of all the ice in the world. In some places the hard-packed snow is over two miles deep.

There is a temptation to exaggerate about Antarctica. And a story seems more dramatic if you tell only one side of it — either telling only of the hardships and dangers, or else of all the modern improvements which have been

13

made. But the whole truth is not that one-sided. Antarctic history is one of heroism and hard living; but it also includes some humor . . . and hope.

Names on the Antarctic map show widely different moods among the men who have explored its secrets. There are places like Desolation Island, Exasperation Inlet, Cape Disappointment, Inexpressible Island and Despair Rock. But other names show a lighter mood: Cape Goodenough, Alamode Island, Precious Peaks and Deliverance Point.

The men on scientific missions in Antarctica today lead a rigorous life. They are crowded into huts or into man-made caves beneath the ice; and for a part of each year they are virtual prisoners on the continent. Yet their morale is high, and they take pride in their work. They are absolutely vain about the long beards which can be produced during an Antarctic winter; and few of the veterans will hesitate to poke good-natured fun at young newcomers. A favorite gag is to sell them bottles of "100-year-old water" — which anybody can get just by melting snow from far below the surface.

The Antarctic climate is awful; and the fact that the men live there now all year round doesn't change this a bit. The wind is so strong that it once ripped a twin-engined DC-3 airplane free of its tie-down cables and simply blew it away. Three days later the fliers, who had weathered out the storm in a nearby base, found the plane 10 miles away — near the top of a 350-foot ice cliff.

Antarctica is cold, too. On the average, it is 30 degrees colder than the comparable area around the North Pole. A quick, careless breath can freeze a man's lungs. The temperature may rise or fall almost 100 degrees within a few weeks, but there are only a few sections of Antarctica where it ever goes above freezing.

Surprisingly enough, the snowfall in Antarctica is

rather light. If the few inches of fresh snow which fall there each year were converted into rain, Antarctica would rank as one of the driest places on earth. When wind strikes the old snow which has been accumulating for centuries, however, the effect is much the same as any ordinary blizzard.

Most of Antarctica is covered with ice, yet water is scarce.

Yet there are "oases" in Antarctica. There are unfrozen lakes and huge areas of snow-free ground. The mystery of how they got there is no more puzzling than the origin of Antarctica itself; for there is clear proof that the continent was once blessed with a mild climate which encouraged the growth of forests and flowers. What happened? The reason for the change and why the oases remain is one of the questions Antarctic scientists would like to solve.

No Eskimos live there. The only "natives" are in the form of plant and animal life, which now is skimpy on the continent itself although still rich and colorful in the waters around it. But Antarctica itself has plenty of natural wonders — volcanoes, rock gorges and huge frozen rivers 30 miles wide. There is color, too. Ice can split up the light like a prism, and white snow may reflect delicate shades of pink, purple and blue. It is a pretty place.

Mount Erebus, near the edge of the Ross Ice Shelf, is the only volcano on the continent still active.

The side of an iceberg shows remains of a camp built by Admiral Byrd more than 20 years earlier, when the ice was still locked securely to the continent.

Antarctica is difficult to reach, and man has taken a while to roll back its frontiers. Its surface is dotted with "ghost towns" — bases which once were manned but which now have been surrendered again to nature. In some cases the drifting snows have blotted out man's traces completely, covering even the high radio masts erected by the pioneers of this century. Other old camps have been pushed right off the continent; they were built on the ice shelves which move slowly but inevitably toward the sea until their edges split off to form icebergs.

These enormous ice islands are a constant threat to vessels approaching Antarctica. Even a relatively small iceberg can rip open the bottom of a ship, for most of the berg floats below the waterline and its jagged sides are almost as unyielding as rock. However, many icebergs dwarf the largest ships — or even a whole flotilla — by comparison. Once an Antarctic patrol sighted an iceberg which was 208 miles long and 60 miles wide — larger in area than the whole country of Belgium.

Approaching ships must pick a path through the icebergs.

Time has strange meanings in the Antarctic. To begin with, the continent is in the Southern Hemisphere, so that its warmest months come when cities like New York and Paris are having winter. But that's not all. For a good part of each year there is 24-hour daylight; then for several months the bulk of the continent is draped in constant night. And at the very bottom of the earth all the time bands come together, so that a clock there is never wrong . . . but is never really right either. Directions are confusing, too. When you are right at the South Pole, any direction you face is north.

To simplify matters, men at the South Pole have agreed to use New Zealand time. They have also made up their own mapping system, which pretends that you are looking north only when you face Greenwich, England. "South" is then at your back.

If all this seems confusing and artificial, don't let it worry you. Existence in Antarctica *is* artificial. Heat, food, building supplies and even the residents have all been imported. Man stays there only through sheer, stubborn determination.

Nevertheless there are good reasons why many nations have scientific stations there. The Antarctic is teaching us the history and geography of the earth. It is an excellent place to study certain aspects of space. Someday it may even be a springboard to the planets. It can help us to understand much of the world's weather, and Antarctic minerals may eventually figure in world commerce.

No book — certainly no short one — can tell you everything there is to know about a whole continent. The best it can offer is an honest, up-to-date outline. Hopefully, it will feature the right highlights in the right proportions. Part of this book deals with history, because it is hard to appreciate today's exploits in Antarctica without understanding some of the difficulties of the past. Several chapters describe the way modern Antarcticans live, travel and work. Science is mentioned throughout, because most of what we know about Antarctica and most of what goes on there now can be traced to scientific curiosity.

And what about tomorrow? Icebreakers, airplanes and atomic power are revolutionizing life in Antarctica. Within this generation the number of people who have visited the continent may reach the hundreds of thousands. It is their ideas and their efforts which will shape the future of this still largely unknown land.

CHAPTER TWO

The Approach by Sea

The ancient Greek scholars who gave Antarctica its name were thoughtful, orderly and imaginative. Being thoughtful, they reasoned to the fact that the earth was a sphere. Being orderly, they decided there must be land at the bottom of the globe as well as at the top — to keep it balanced. Being imaginative, they based their name for the far-off southern continent on a picture they invented in the night sky. *Arktikos* is the Greek word for "bear," and this is what they called a particular group of stars which were always in the northern heavens. Land on the other side of the world was clearly "opposite the bear," so they called it just that. The Greek name was *Antarktikos,* and they showed it on their maps.

That's where the Greeks stopped, however. They never tried to visit the bottom of the earth.

Legends among the islanders just west of Tahiti say that a Polynesian hero named Ui-te-Rangiora visited the frozen southern seas in a canoe during the seventh century A.D. If this is true his brave crew must have been good paddlers, because the Ross Sea of Antarctica is more than 2,000 miles due south of Rarotonga. Perhaps they were, but we will probably never know for sure. They left no specific records of their journey.

Once Columbus showed the world that oceans could be crossed safely, it was just a matter of time before men would visit the Antarctic. At first the merchant sailors stuck to Magellan's route around the tip of South America, staying clear of icy waters to the south unless they were driven off course by unkind winds. But in the mid-eighteenth century a series of French daredevils (their names were Bouvet, Kerguelen and Dufresne) sailed south deliberately to look for new territory. They found islands — pretty poor ones at that — but no continent.

In 1772, British Captain James Cook began a three-year voyage that was to take him and both his ships all around Antarctica, but never in sight of it. Nevertheless, his explorations on this and other voyages were important. First, he proved that New Zealand and Australia were not connected to any land mass in the south. Second, he decided that if an Antarctic continent existed it must be completely barren and incredibly cold. Finally, when he discovered the island of South Georgia, Cook noted in his log that its beaches were crowded with fur seals. That casual report is what really triggered the "rush to Antarctica," which reached a climax in the 1820's.

Sealskins could be sold in China those days for as much as $20 apiece. And the beaches of a few southern islands were so crowded with seals that the creatures had to be chased away to make room to drag a rowboat ashore.

Gradually American and British hunters pushed southward, and perhaps some of the early sealers reached the Antarctic coast itself. But they were as secretive as a bunch of gold miners, and they kept any discoveries to themselves.

There is a great dispute over who first *reported* a true sighting of the continent. It may have been young Nathaniel B. Palmer, a Connecticut Yankee from Stonington. This boy of twenty commanded a sealing sloop less than half as big as Columbus' flagship; and in November, 1820, he almost definitely sighted the mainland. Earlier in the same year, however, a British naval commander named Edward Bransfield had visited the same area; and he may also have caught a glimpse of the coast.

The 1820–21 season was a busy one. About thirty U.S. ships visited the area, near the west coast of the Antarctic Peninsula, and the eight vessels in Captain Palmer's group alone collected 10,000 seal pelts in 12 days.

The first sealers to arrive usually took over the choicest hunting grounds, while later ships had to search for herds elsewhere. So it was that Captain John Davis and his three-masted vessel from New Haven sailed farther and farther south that year until finally he put a small boat ashore on the Antarctic continent itself. The first landing (in February, 1821) was probably made on the coast of Hughes Bay, near the northernmost tip of Antarctica. The men stayed ashore less than an hour; and, although Captain Davis guessed correctly that the towering snow-covered landscape was the edge of a new continent, he was disappointed. Why? . . . Because there were no seals around.

Before long, this was the situation all over the Antarctic. Fur seals made no effort to escape the hunters; and they were easy to kill. All a hunter had to do was give one a clout on the nose. Within two years after Palmer's voyage, the breed had almost vanished; and the Antarctic hunters turned to elephant seals and whales instead.

Some whaling firms encouraged their captains to explore, but for the next few years the most important discoveries came from the navies of France, Great Britain and the United States. In 1839 and 1840, for example, U. S. Navy Lieutenant Charles Wilkes sailed along the Antarctic coast about 1,500 miles. He sighted land repeatedly, and such a long stretch of shoreline proved that the newly discovered territory was indeed a continent.

However, Wilkes' little wooden fleet was hardly equipped for this sort of exploration. None of the six ships was fortified against the ice; and the freezing, stinging sea swept onto the decks through the large open gun ports. Furthermore, storage space was lacking for the provisions needed on such a long journey; the group soon ran low on food. To top things off, Wilkes was somewhat of a tyrant; and almost a quarter of his crew deserted before the voyage was over.

Wilkes missed by about 100 miles in calculating the latitudes of the Antarctic coast he saw, and his enemies used this as an excuse to throw doubt on his whole report. His bitter crewmen were quite willing to discredit him, and some even testified that they hadn't seen the Antarctic continent at all. Wilkes was brought before a court-martial, but acquitted.

Fortunately, the rash charges did not ruin Lieutenant Wilkes' career, and he went on to become an admiral. Modern studies show that his drawings and chartings of the coastline were essentially accurate. Whatever his personality was like, his name as an important Antarctic explorer is safe.

The foremost British explorer of that period, James Ross, had better luck. Ross had had experience in the Far North, and his expedition was much more sensibly equipped than Wilkes'. His two ships were strongly built, and reinforced by extra timbers. Each hull had a double coating of copper, and the interior walls were watertight. With ships like these, Ross could afford to be bold. He sailed south, right into the ice pack.

For four days the ships threaded their way between icebergs or through narrow "leads" (cracks in the ice pack). Then came an astonishing sight — a rich blue expanse of open sea.

Ross was in for more surprises as he sailed southward for hundreds of miles through the sea which now bears his name. He saw shores lined with ice; but he also saw rocky, snow-free land. Finally, he came upon two giant volcanoes. Imagine the sight of smoke pouring from a 12,000-foot crater in the midst of such an icy wilderness.

Discovery of the 200-foot-high Ross Ice Barrier ended early hopes of sailing to the South Pole.

Another man might have become poetic, but Ross was a down-to-earth type. He named the volcanoes for his two ships — the larger Erebus, and its companion Terror.

By this time Ross had reached the site of what would become the largest "city" in Antarctica, McMurdo Sound. He was near the starting point for the first overland trips to the South Pole itself. And he was sailing across water which, when frozen, would someday support a mighty fleet of cargo planes. But Ross was near the end of his southward voyage. Up ahead was a solid wall of ice, as tall as a 20-story building. This was no mere iceberg, or even a glacier. It was a shelf of ice the size of Texas, so firmly attached to the continent that it is still shown on some maps as part of the land mass. More than two generations would pass before any man could come closer to

the bottom of the world, and Ross had done the best that could ever be done by sea.

People seemed to forget about Antarctica for a while after the voyages of Ross, Wilkes and the Frenchman d'Urville (who explored the Australian side of the continental coast during the same period). Matthew Maury, a commander in the U. S. Navy, tried to encourage many nations to study the Antarctic simultaneously in 1860; but the U. S. Civil War canceled that plan. In 1874, however, the growing interest in science revived interest in the area. A U. S. expedition was landed on Kerguelen Island in order to get a good view of the planet Venus as it came close to the earth that year. And a British ship called *Challenger,* making a trip around the world to investigate the oceans scientifically, became the first steam-powered vessel to cross the Antarctic Circle.

Whalers soon found that steam engines had definite advantages over sails. They were fast and they were sure. Still, few Antarctic ships switched completely to steam until the 1930's. And before then, the small engines which were added to sailpower were sometimes just enough to get the ships into trouble . . . yet not enough to get them out.

In 1897 the Belgians sent a steam-sail ship, the *Belgica,* to explore Antarctica under the command of Lieutenant Adrien de Gerlache. In a way, it was an international expedition. Norwegian Roald Amundsen was first mate; and Frederic Cook, an American, was medical officer. When the time came for the *Belgica* to return, she found herself stuck fast in the ice. The weak, inefficient engines couldn't break her free, and the whole party drifted for a year with the ice pack.

Later the same thing happened to several other expeditions. In a couple of cases the wooden ships were crushed like orange crates as the ice closed in. Yet sailors were

Admiral Byrd's ship *Bear*
was called "the strongest wooden ship ever built."

afraid that thin steel hulls might be ripped or torn by
jagged ice; and it was not until Richard E. Byrd's expedition in 1929 that the first steel-hulled exploration ship
ventured into the Antarctic. As if to show that he wasn't
breaking completely with the past, however, Byrd also
used a wooden vessel, rigged with sails.

Antarctic ship styles changed drastically in the course
of numerous expeditions by Byrd and others during the
next 25 years. By the mid-1940's, sea transportation had
reached an advanced stage; and the ships which have

27

USS *Atka* looks like an ant with an enormous crumb as it nudges a three-billion-pound iceberg out of the shipping channel at Mc-Murdo Sound.

visited Antarctica since then look quite different from the ones which first made history there.

In fact, the icebreakers — the ships which lead modern Antarctic convoys — don't look much like anything else you can imagine. Their hulls are shaped almost like barrels. This construction keeps them from being crushed by the ice pack, even if they are caught fast. As the ice presses inward, the round bottom of the ship simply pops up like a marble.

Most people think that an icebreaker *cuts* into ice, and they imagine such a ship as having a very sharp bow. Actually this isn't so. The icebreaker gets a running start and forces its blunt nose right up onto the ice, crushing it with the sheer weight of the ship.

As it approaches its destination on the continent, the icebreaker must chop out a berth in the ice for each of the cargo ships or tankers which follow it. With short, deft runs it will carve open an area which matches the contour of each supply vessel. The ice alongside each berth will become the "pier" — the unloading platform for men and cargo. For this reason, the ice area selected for a berth must be relatively smooth, firmly connected to the shore, and free of cracks or flaws which might make it break up during the landing operation.

Icebreakers themselves have changed somewhat in recent years. Some used to have an extra propeller in front, designed to suck water out from under the ice sheet just ahead. This made it easier to crack the ice, and it also forced the ice splinters away from the sides of the ship. The front propeller was constantly being damaged, however, so it is no longer used in thick sea ice. Nevertheless, the front of an icebreaker still has a step to it — just like the rear. This step, added originally to house the stem of the propeller, gives the edge of the ice pack an extra jolt

The stubby shape of an icebreaker (*left*) is shown clearly here at Port Lyttleton, New Zealand, where U. S. convoys assemble for Antarctic voyages.

as the ship glides forward. It also keeps the icebreaker from riding up too far onto the ice.

Occasionally, of course, even a powerful icebreaker may get stuck. When this happened to a ship in the old days, the captain would simply order his crew to run back and forth from one side of the ship to the other. This started a rocking motion which would usually permit it to break free. Now things are a bit easier on the seamen; every modern icebreaker is equipped with interconnecting tanks — at the front and rear, and on both sides. Seawater is pumped into the tanks, then back and forth between them. The shifting of the water helps an icebound ship to rock itself loose.

An icebreaker is a clumsy, lurching vessel to watch or to ride on. In the open sea it has no keel to stabilize it, and it may roll 40 degrees to one side or the other, even in a calm sea. In the ice pack, however, it proves its worth. Approaching the heavy white sheet like a mean little bulldog, it will roar off first to the left, twisting and grinding to a halt until the ice splits and the whole ship comes crashing down as if the sea had been pulled out from under it. Then the ship will back off and come smashing forward again, this time to the right. It is a rough, start-and-stop ride. But unless channels were broken like this for ordinary ships to use, it would be impossible to reach some parts of the Antarctic coast with the large amounts of bulky supplies needed by modern operations. In fact, it would be impossible to reach some parts of the coast at all.

The largest icebreaker in the Antarctic today is a U. S. Navy ship called the *Glacier*. It is as long as a football field and almost as wide. Some of the first ships to approach the Antarctic would fit neatly on its helicopter deck.

The *Glacier's* size and the force of its 10 diesel-electric

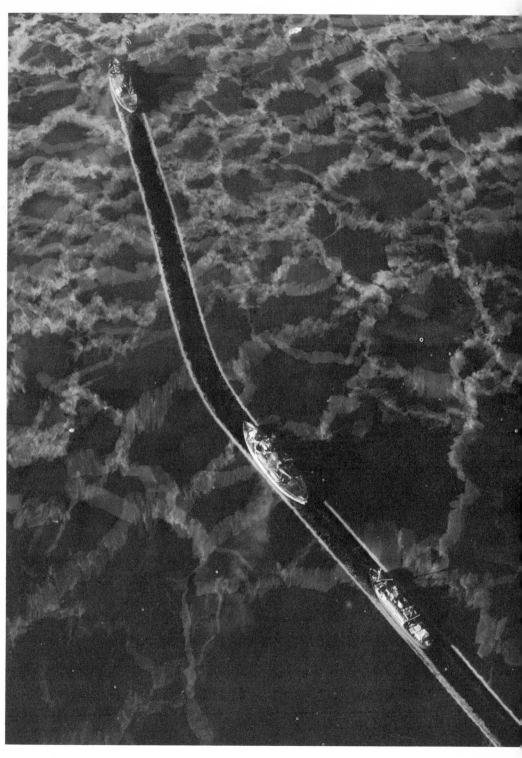

Two icebreakers and a transport ship push through a relatively thin ice pack near the northernmost tip of Antarctica.

engines enable it to break through ice 15 feet thick. It is more than 100 times as powerful as the first ship used by Byrd, and immensely more useful than the tiny wooden vessels of the early sealers.

Following the icebreakers are the "payload carriers" of the modern Antarctic fleet — cargo vessels, tankers and research ships. Some of them are ordinary ships which have simply been strengthened by extra plates, especially near the bow. Others, however, are designed especially for service in the icy Antarctic. Usually such a ship has a reinforced hull, a sloping bow, and very powerful engines. The controls are normally located in the crow's nest at the very top of the ship, so that the captain can plot his course far ahead through the ice.

Many nations now have ships of this type. Some are used chiefly to deliver the expedition groups themselves. Others, like the United States' tanker *Chattahoochee,* may shuttle back and forth several times during a single season, delivering more than a million gallons of gasoline and diesel oil on each trip. The Russian vessels *Ob* and *Lena* carry on scientific research as they steam through the Antarctic Ocean; and the American *Eltanin* is actually a floating laboratory.

The *Eltanin* studies ocean currents, marine biology, weather and even cosmic rays. Unlike the ancient Greeks who gave Antarctica its name, scientists of today are not content to sit at home and guess what the rest of the world is like. They want to get the facts about nature on the spot.

There is still exploring to be done in the Antarctic — not only on land, but also along the coast. The continent has been circled many times; but the unmelting ice pack in some areas is so thick that no ship has yet been able to move in close enough to chart the shorelines.

As recently as 1961, a pair of U. S. Navy icebreakers

A balloon is launched from the U. S. research ship *Eltanin*.

visited one section of the "phantom coast" for the first time. In doing so, they proved that one large "peninsula" on Antarctic maps was really an island. Venturing into the very area of the Bellingshausen Sea, where de Gerlache's expedition had been trapped for a year, the *Glacier* and a smaller ship nearly became locked into the ice pack themselves. Ice in this region, which is southwest of South America, is so thick that sunlight cannot penetrate it. Samples of the seawater beneath show that — unlike other parts of the Antarctic Ocean — it is relatively empty of marine life.

Winds of 100 miles an hour lashed the two ships, and ropes on deck turned into heavy chains of ice. Frozen spray transformed masts into icicles and molded deck equipment into grotesque statues, so that the crew members had to break away the ice with pick-axes and heavy wooden sledgehammers just to keep operating. In heavy Antarctic storms, some ships have picked up as much as 1,000 tons of ice in layers up to 10 feet thick. A load like that could cause a top-heavy, round-bottomed icebreaker to capsize; and the 1961 expedition involved many close calls.

Once, when the icebreakers were stuck fast in the pack but a channel was spotted in the distance, 1,500 pounds of explosives had to be set off to help clear a passageway to open water. It worked. Ordinarily, however, the pressure which builds up in the ice under a heavy wind is so great that it can keep any ship pinned securely; even explosives don't help. It may be possible to break the ice directly ahead of the ship, but there is no way to shove the shattered chunks out of the way. The only thing to do in a case like this is to wait until the wind changes or dies down. Once during this particular trip the mighty *Glacier* was locked in the pack for four days before a sudden, unexplained shift enabled her to build up speed again and crunch her way to freedom — with the smaller icebreaker steaming close behind her.

This voyage and others like it prove that we still have much to learn about Antarctica. A whole mountain range which had appeared on maps for years was nowhere to be seen when the *Glacier* approached one little-known section of the coast. The area which mountains were sup-

Sailors remove ice from the superstructure of USS *Burton Island* after an Antarctic storm.

posed to occupy was nothing but an empty ice shelf. Parts of the actual coast were then charted, but the weather was so bad that the job could not be completed. Even on the latest maps, many areas are still drawn with dotted lines, indicating that geographers are uncertain about them. Other ships and other explorers have their work cut out for them.

Compared with the voyages of the nineteenth century,

today's sea trips to the Antarctic are luxurious. The food is good and there is plenty of it. Cabins are warm and comfortable; and recreation is provided by movies and books. Most important of all, however, is the fact that modern ships are powerful enough to cruise safely through most Antarctic waters. To a great extent, man has conquered the last of the seven seas.

Dog sleds are still favored by some Antarctic travelers.

CHAPTER THREE

Destination – South Pole

When a new mountain is discovered, there are some men who cannot rest until it has been climbed. Once the Antarctic continent was found, adventurous men were bound to try to cross it. Each hoped to be the first to stand at the very bottom of the earth.

Until space probes made it possible to see the other side of the moon, many people had the romantic idea that the far side would be different from the drab, lifeless surface we always see. Antarctica aroused the same kind of curiosity. What lay beyond its icy coastal mountains? Was the interior just as bleak? Would there be any evidence of warmth or life? Might there be exciting new horizons to cross . . . new mountains to climb?

The first great effort came at the opening of the twentieth century. In August, 1901, a young British naval officer named Robert F. Scott sailed from England in command of a Royal Society expedition which was to last three full years. After making sure that no sea passage led through the Ross Ice Shelf, Scott's group made camp at McMurdo Sound. Since the purpose of the expedition was exclusively scientific study, no attempt was made on this trip to reach the Pole; but the men built up valuable experience in overland travel.

Scott experimented with dog sleds and finally decided that it would be better for the men to haul the sledges themselves. The dogs had huge appetites, but there was no wild game in the interior of the continent to fill out their diet. Scott was unwilling either to carry along extra provisions or to drive some of the dogs to death and let the rest turn cannibal (a practice which some explorers followed) .

In 1902, Scott and two companions trudged more than 300 miles directly south across the ice shelf, reaching a line of mountains and glaciers which swung southeastward in the general direction of the Pole. Later they climbed another glacier close to McMurdo Sound and became the first to explore the broad, smooth plateau which covers most of the continent, and on which the Pole itself is located.

Short rations and heavy exertion made most of these first "traverses" miserable for Scott's party, but in one case they got a pleasant surprise. On their way down from the polar plateau they stumbled into a sheltered snow-free valley. They found a lake, a little stream, and warmer weather than they had felt anywhere else in Antarctica. This meant little in planning for a trip to the center of the continent, however. Scott was fairly sure now that the Pole was on a plateau more than a mile and a half above sea level, unprotected from the wind by mountain walls and too high to offer any hope of an oasis like this. The journey to the ultimate south would be a cold, lonely one.

Strangely enough, the first to try the long trek itself was Ernest Shackleton — a big, jovial Irishman who had started the 1901–1904 trip with Scott while only a teenager, but who had been sent home then because his health had broken under the strain. Shackleton yearned to make up for what he considered a humiliation, and by 1908 he had collected enough money to begin his own expedition. Because he promised Scott that he would not use the hut they had built on the earlier trip, Shackleton made camp at Cape Royds, some 20 miles away. This was near the foot of Mount Erebus; and — despite a blizzard — three members of Shackleton's party became the first men to climb to the top of the smoking, rumbling volcano. The climb must have taken almost superhuman effort. There is so little oxygen at such altitude that it is practically impossible to start a fire. The climbers had to gasp for air; and the water vapor from their heavy breathing turned into ice crystals, which crackled in the air and coated the fronts of their parkas with a layer of frost. Near the peak, the smell of sulfur was stifling. Yet the joy of success at reaching the top was like a tonic. Forgetting caution, they raced back down the slope, slithering over the icy surface like boys on a sliding board.

At the beginning of the next Antarctic summer, one group from Shackleton's party started off toward the South Magnetic Pole while he and others prepared for the attack on the geographic Pole. The first goal was reached on January 16, 1909. Professor Edgeworth David, Dr. A. F. Mackay and Sir Douglas Mawson, of Australia, reached the precise spot toward which all magnetic compass needles dip. They marked the location with a British flag and headed happily back toward Cape Royds.

It should be noted that the magnetic poles of the earth are constantly changing. The movement doesn't matter much to a navigator in the temperate zones, but near the ends of the earth the effect is astonishing. Since 1909 the South Magnetic Pole has shifted about eight miles toward the northwest each year, and today it is no longer even on the mainland of Antarctica.

The *geographic* South Pole is what Shackleton himself was after, however. This is the "bottom of the world," the place on all our globes at which the lines of longitude come together.

Like Scott, Shackleton decided against using dog sleds. Instead, he tried an automobile on skis; but this proved a waste of time. The machine bogged down immediately. Then he turned to the sturdy little Siberian ponies he had brought with him. They had drawbacks too, however. Unlike dogs, they couldn't eat the same sort of food the men ate — making the problem of provisions worse than ever. Furthermore, although they were accustomed to a cold climate, the ponies' fine manes could not shield them from the biting, powdery snow of an Antarctic blizzard. Shackleton killed several of the ponies for food, and by the time the group had struggled up the mighty river of ice called the Beardmore Glacier the men were pulling the sledges themselves.

Shackleton and his men could probably have reached the Pole; they came within 97 miles of it. But even the optimistic Irishman knew that he would be pressing his luck if he did not turn back. Sixty-seven days had passed since the group had left the main camp, and they could expect the weather to get worse. On the return trip each man would be limited to a cup of tea, a small pot of stew and a biscuit or two a day. Shackleton was a brave leader but a wisely cautious one. The prize of the Pole was left for others to win.

Scott's turn came again three seasons later. This time he plotted and scheduled every move precisely. He would follow the same route as Shackleton, leaving stores of food and fuel along his way to the Pole so that he could use them on the trip back. Taking no chances, he resolved to try more than one form of transportation. He started out this time with dogs, ponies and three motor-driven sledges.

A less determined man than Scott might have let his careful plans be upset by the news he received on his way to Antarctica that year. The Norwegian explorer Roald Amundsen had gathered funds to support an expedition to the North Pole, but the American Robert Peary beat him to the goal, reaching it in 1909. Amundsen, who had

Motor sledges have been used
in some form for more than half a century.

already been the first to sail through the Northwest Passage across the upper edge of Canada, was never satisfied with second place. Without any formal announcement to his backers or even to his crew, Amundsen decided on his own to tackle the south polar trip which had not yet been accomplished. He sent a personal message to Scott to let him know that he too was heading for Antarctica.

Scott refused to be coaxed into a race. He knew that Amundsen would travel a slightly shorter route and that he would use lightweight dog sleds. If the Norwegian made it to the Pole at all, he would certainly get there first. But Scott was intent on following his original schedule, including various scientific studies which he had promised to perform. He was like a runner who ignores all competition and concentrates entirely on his own form and timing.

Scott's luck couldn't have been worse. Storms delayed his arrival in Antarctica until January, 1911. Then he set out across the ice to establish a large supply depot which would be his final stop on the return trek the following season. Although January is part of the Antarctic summer, the weather was as bad as any Scott had seen, and he was forced to drop his stores 36 miles short of the intended site.

After wintering at Cape Evans, near McMurdo Sound, Scott was ready to begin the great adventure. Unfortunately, his motor sleds were destined to fail. One had already been lost in a crevasse, and by the time the party reached the first supply base the other two had died with cracked cylinders. Then — just a day's march short of the Beardmore Glacier — the whole group was pinned down by a four-day blizzard. When the winds died down and the weather turned warm, the ice and snow melted quickly. Slush tugged at the ponies like quicksand. The animals had to be destroyed; and at the foot of the Beard-

The base from which Scott began his tragic polar march in 1911 has been preserved remarkably by the Antarctic's dry cold.

more Glacier, Scott stuck to his plan by ordering some of his men to return to camp with the dogs. From that point on, it was back to the basic team — tired men pulling heavy sleds. And four more awful blizzards still awaited them.

As Scott and his men passed the point at which Shackleton had turned back, their spirits rose. The weather had finally improved, and the Pole was within easy reach. On January 16, however, their mood of celebration collapsed. Squarely in their path they found a black flag and the remains of a camp. Sled and dog tracks led away to the south. Roald Amundsen had obviously beaten them to the South Pole.

At the Pole itself, they found a Norwegian flag, a tent and a friendly message from Amundsen. He had also left some extra clothing, instruments and a sledge.

With battered bodies and crushed spirits, Scott and his men headed home. None was to make it. One fell and suffered a fatal concussion. A second became so badly frostbitten and ravaged by scurvy that he purposely slipped away from his companions in a storm, preferring suicide to the prospect of slowing them all down. Scott and the other two came within 11 miles of the final food depot, but they could go no farther. Their bodies were discovered eight months later, along with Scott's tragic diary. They had been loyal to their scientific duty to the last, and the trio still had with them the heavy rock specimens they had collected on their final, pathetic traverse.

Roald Amundsen and three of
his companions in a solemn moment at the South Pole.

Amundsen's trip to the Pole seemed deceptively easy by comparison. He had brought an excellent dog handler with him, and all the men spent the winter months on the ice shelf making four extra-lightweight sleds in a room they had hollowed out under the snow. Each sled weighed only about one-third as much as the conventional models they had brought by ship.

Bad weather was a problem during the base-laying operations, but the polar trip itself was made under generally fine conditions. Amundsen and his companions rode the sledges or let themselves be towed on skis for part of the way, thus saving their strength for the rugged and dangerous climb up the Axel Heiberg Glacier. (This was the route the Norwegian had chosen.) Although their plan was to kill most of the dogs along the way in order to ease the supply problem, the group made regular rest stops; and in this way the surviving dogs could stay fresh throughout the trip.

In contrast to Scott's ordeal, some details of the Amundsen expedition were downright lighthearted. When he ran out of trail markers on his depot-laying trips, for instance, Amundsen used dried fish, which stood out clearly against the whiteness. There was no waste, because the fish were perfectly preserved in the 20-below-zero atmosphere and were quite edible later on. Amundsen's food on the trail, incidentally, was both good and ample. On arriving at the Pole, the Norwegians even enjoyed the luxury of celebrating with fine cigars. Nevertheless, a champion in any field can make difficult tasks seem easy. Amundsen was unquestionably a champion explorer, and the fact that he covered the distance from the edge of the continent to the geographic South Pole and back in only 99 days stands as a marvelous example of planning and discipline.

The difficulty of reaching the Pole at all is shown by

The author examines a Sno-Cat
used by Sir Vivian Fuchs to cross the continent.

the fact that no other ground party did so again until the
1957–58 season. That was when Sir Vivian Fuchs and 11
others crossed from the South American side of the
continent to the New Zealand side. Traveling in heated
vehicles, this expedition was aided by some aerial reconnaissance and by constant radio contact with the perma-
ment Antarctic bases. Fuchs' journey across the last 700
miles had the additional advantage that it was made along
a route which had just been marked by Sir Edmund
Hillary, of New Zealand (who actually reached the Pole
before Fuchs). As part of the overall plan, Hillary had
laid down a series of supply depots between that point and
Scott Base (near McMurdo Sound).

A lot of experiments have been made with transportation across ice and snow, but nobody has come up with a
perfect answer yet. The vehicles which move most easily
on a hard ice surface tend to get stuck in soft snow; the

46

type which slogs through snow readily doesn't give the right sort of traction on slick ice. Sir Vivian Fuchs chose vehicles which were long enough to bridge small crevasses, fast enough to whisk across the rough surface without emphasizing each bump, and light enough to keep from breaking through some of the delicate snow bridges they were bound to cross. The motor-driven Sno-Cats which carried the major load for the Commonwealth Expedition of 1957–58 are as light in their tracks as a man on snowshoes. The weight of a big, orange Sno-Cat is so distributed over its four broad treads that it exerts a pressure on the snow of less than one pound per square inch.

These and the other vehicles used in the Antarctic face many problems on a traverse, for even the relatively flat polar plateau is not perfectly smooth. There are hills, and the wind whips snow into waves called sastrugi. These may harden into flint-sharp roadblocks several feet high. In some places, mountains from the very base of the continent also poke through the snow. Isolated peaks, surrounded by ice, are called nunataks; and they present a series of dangerous and dark reminders that the snow surface is . . . just a surface.

The most frightening obstacle of all for an Antarctic traverse is the crevasse. It may be a few feet deep or a few hundred feet, and it can disable man or machine in a moment. Sometimes crevasses are covered by snow; but they can usually be spotted by a soft shadow across the snow, caused by the slight depression. In some cases, however, even this clue is missing.

Far to the north, Alpine mountain climbers have grown accustomed to the danger of crevasses. Members of a climbing group in Switzerland will rope themselves together for protection, and the lead man may carry a long, light pole with which to test the surface ahead. If the snow is solid, the thin staff will penetrate only a few feet; but if the traveler is on the brink of a crevasse his pole will break through the snow bridge which covers it. This means slow going, of course; so modern travel in the Antarctic borrows the principles but speeds up the process.

The lead vehicle pushes before it a fan-shaped framework. At the front of each prong is a metal dish which looks like an oversized salad bowl. Each of these electronic detectors is tuned to the normal properties of hard-packed snow and ice, so that a gap in the solid crust will disturb the electrical current and flash a warning signal inside the Sno-Cat. As an extra precaution, each vehicle in the "swing" or caravan may be tied securely to the next one in line. Steel wire is also looped around each vehicle, so that it will be easier to pull out if it gets into trouble. Finally, an escape hatch is built into the roof of most tractor cabs. This final safety measure has saved the lives of several men whose vehicles broke through sea ice and plunged out of sight within seconds. It has also aided the rescue of drivers who found themselves teetering on the edge of a deep crevasse.

Smaller trail groups sometimes use motor toboggans. One of these low-slung mechanical workhorses can seat two passengers and pull a ton of supplies; but the men who use them rarely choose to ride. Fearing crevasses, a driver can operate the controls by tugging on 60-foot reins. He and his teammate are pulled along on skis well behind the toboggan.

The mechanization of Antarctic travel came gradually. Admiral Richard E. Byrd, who later thrilled the world with an airplane flight over the Pole, favored motor transport from the start. He took two tractors with him on his very first U. S. expedition in 1928. They didn't perform as well as he had hoped; but he felt certain that in time they would replace dog sleds. Following Amundsen's lead (although not all the way to the Pole), Byrd's trail parties explored and re-explored the interior of Antarctica — using dogs, for the time being. On one occasion his men actually recovered a five-gallon can of kerosene, some matches, and a note which Amundsen had left inside a rock-pile marker 18 years before. In the same way, the Byrd expedition left notes which were to be found decades later by the men who followed them.

On his next Antarctic trip, Byrd used three tractor trucks to set up the remote weather base he was to occupy all by himself for four months. This time they proved their worth; and in fact they saved his life. Fumes from a leaky stove began to poison Byrd in his tiny cubbyhole, but he needed the heat to survive and he was unwilling to risk his friends' lives by asking them to come to his rescue in the dark of winter. The men back at Byrd's main base could tell from his unsteady radio messages that he was seriously ill, however; and despite the 64-below-zero cold they sent out a tractor with floodlights to reach the lonely outpost. When the rescue party arrived Byrd was on the verge of death; but, thanks to the mechanized equipment, they had arrived in time to save him.

In 1939, Byrd showed again that his ideas were ahead of his time. He arrived in Antarctica with a light tank (which worked fairly well in the snow) and an enormous

Byrd's Snow Cruiser was underpowered, but it was the forerunner of large, useful motor-driven vehicles in Antarctica.

vehicle which he called the Snow Cruiser. The four-man house-on-wheels was bigger than a bus and even had a small airplane mounted on its roof. Its tires were more than nine feet high. Like the dinosaurs of old, however, the vehicle was too big for its own good. Its weight caused the tires to gouge deep ruts in the snow, and the Snow Cruiser had barely enough power to move along the trail. Today, the Snow Cruiser's successors hum busily back and forth at bases all over Antarctica. More powerful engines make the huge American D-9 tractors an important factor in loading, hauling and construction projects — in spite of the fact that each one of these giants weighs more than 75,000 pounds. They move about on treads four and a half feet wide.

In the mid-1950's, the United States decided to set up a permanent station more than 500 miles east of Byrd's

Drivers walk behind two
D-9 tractors, steering them by wire controls.

old weather base. To get there with large construction equipment, Army trail experts had to mark out a safe path across miles of ice which was crisscrossed with crevasses. The worst section of all was nicknamed "Fashion Lane." It was almost a spider web of deep crevasses. With care, the narrower gaps could be crossed; but other crevasses were far too wide. Exploring the great underlying ice caves one by one, the road builders used high explosives to collapse the walls of each crevasse. Then bulldozers would scrape snow and ice fragments along the surface and dump them into the holes until they were filled. "Army-Navy Drive," as the men called it, was marked by colored flags and empty fuel drums. Appropriately, the station they set up at the end of it was named for Admiral Richard E. Byrd.

A few years later, when the United States sent its first two overland expeditions to the South Pole, the trail parties didn't attempt such a thorough job. Taking advantage of good aerial reconnaissance, they simply detoured around the worst crevasse fields.

Travel across the emptiness of Antarctica is still difficult; but much of its original uncertainty has disappeared. Little houses called wanigans are now mounted on sleds which are towed along behind the big tractors. Cooking was a difficult chore for Scott and his band, but today each snow train carries its own small kitchen. Fuel is as important as food, so some of the caravans now include "rolli-tankers," whose oversized balloon tires are filled with gasoline or diesel fuel. The pace of a modern scientific traverse still leaves little time to relax, however. The men are on the trail from 14 to 16 hours a day, not counting a couple of hours extra spent to keep the vehicles in good working order.

The vehicles being used now in Antarctica are remarkably hardy. In 1962, a special party from McMurdo Sound

Modern snow tractors are used in scientific excursions.

located several tractors, a Sno-Cat and a couple of Trax-cavators which had been left at two outlying bases six years earlier. It took some clever field repair work, but all of them were cleared of snow and put back into running order. Then the "mobile junkyard" chugged back to McMurdo under its own power, saving the taxpayers about $300,000 in replacement costs.

Still, there are diehards who argue that such "gas burners" can never replace dog sleds. The New Zealanders use huskies to a considerable extent, and claim that the dogs will always be needed in Antarctic areas where the snow is spotted with bare, rocky ground. Sled pulling is not really such hard work for the big dogs, incidentally; and they seem to enjoy it.

Sir Vivian Fuchs used dog teams as advance scouts during most of his transcontinental expedition, but once he got to the Pole he asked American authorities to fly them back to Scott Base. He found that they slowed him down in open country.

To drivers who always stay within easy towing distance of a garage, moving across Antarctica in complicated, temperamental machines might seem foolhardy. Gasoline becomes syrupy, rubber hoses crack in the cold, and even metal becomes brittle. But necessity makes excellent mechanics even better. Major repair jobs have been carried out in sub-zero weather with such unusual replacement parts as metal studs, building nails and baling wire.

The largest vehicles being used for cross-country travel in Antarctica today belong to the Russians. They used

The Russian Kharkov Chankas are big and fast.

Building materials and equipment were dropped by parachute to enable a U. S. group to establish a permanent station at the geographic South Pole in 1956.

35-ton snow tractors on a visit to Amundsen-Scott base as early at 1959. These Kharkov Chankas are almost as big as Byrd's Snow Cruiser, but they are much more highly powered. Their supercharged 12-cylinder engines develop 1,000 horsepower each.

The Russian vehicles are air-conditioned and comfortable, but they seem almost overly elaborate on the inside. The walls are covered with green synthetic leather, and there is brown linoleum on the floors. Foam-rubber armchairs, table lamps, curtain-covered portholes and a shower stall round out the homelike touches. Like the American Sno-Cats, the vehicles carry bunks and cooking facilities. A transparent observation dome in the roof enables the navigator aboard to check the sun's position without even stepping outside.

The comparative comfort of a modern Antarctic traverse would probably be very surprising to the early Antarctic explorers. They would be even more amazed, no doubt, that the South Pole itself is no longer deserted. All sorts of activity is mirrored in the shiny glass ball atop an orange and black bamboo pole which marks (approximately) the bottom of the earth. All year round, scientists there carry on studies of weather, cosmic rays, and other aspects of the upper atmosphere. The permanent station which was set up by airlift in 1956 is named Amundsen-Scott Station, in honor of the first two great polar explorers. Believe it or not, it is the site of an annual football game. Every Thanksgiving Day, the Navy Seabees play the research scientists in a full, 60-minute "Ice Bowl" classic.

Despite all the progress which has been made since 1901, however, the map showing Antarctic traverses is still almost as clear as the snow of the polar plateau. Only a few thin lines stretch across the great expanses of territory on which no man has ever set foot. There is still room for new Antarctic pioneers.

Using a basketball (the best substitute on hand in 1962) the sailors kick off to the scientists in the first annual football game at the South Pole.

CHAPTER FOUR

Where Did It Come From?

What is the continent like? Underneath its heavy cloak of ice, what is the shape and appearance of Antarctica? Was it always an empty, cruel wilderness? . . . and will it always remain so?

Only 200 miles from the South Pole, men have scratched a hole in the side of a mountain. It doesn't look too impressive, but it is the southernmost coal mine in the world. The scientists who dug it aren't interested in using the coal for fires . . . although they would welcome the extra heat. They simply want to find out how the coal got there. And, in a way, they want to learn how Antarctica got there.

Coal like this took many millions of years to form. It began with trees and ferns, which died and were buried in swamps. Instead of rotting away into dust, the plants were pressed down with great force until heat and pressure gradually converted them into the hard, shiny blueblack chunks we call coal.

This mine is near the peak
of a mountain surrounded by snow fields thousands of feet deep.

The obvious question in Antarctica is: "Where did the plants come from?" Anybody who looks across the flat wastes of the polar plateau finds it hard to imagine that a rain forest once existed in this same spot.

There is even more specific evidence that it did, however. Some of the lumps of coal show the outlines of fern leaves. And in the same neighborhood are pieces of petrified wood — whole logs which have been turned into stone by a different natural process. There is no doubt that forests of palm and pine trees once grew in Antarctica. There were sequoias too, as well as beech trees — and even figs.

The earth hasn't always had the same climate. It has gone through cold spells, when glaciers covered the United States as far south as Kentucky. And there have been warmer periods, when the ice caps at the poles were much smaller than they are now. But it doesn't seem likely that the ice has ever vanished completely since life began on earth.

This leaves two clear possibilities. Either the South Pole has moved, or Antarctica has moved. Probably both are true.

First, consider the Poles themselves. Imagine that you are looking down at the earth from a point in space high above either the North or the South Pole. The earth would look like a wheel, spinning around on a tiny axle. The spot at the very center, the only spot that doesn't

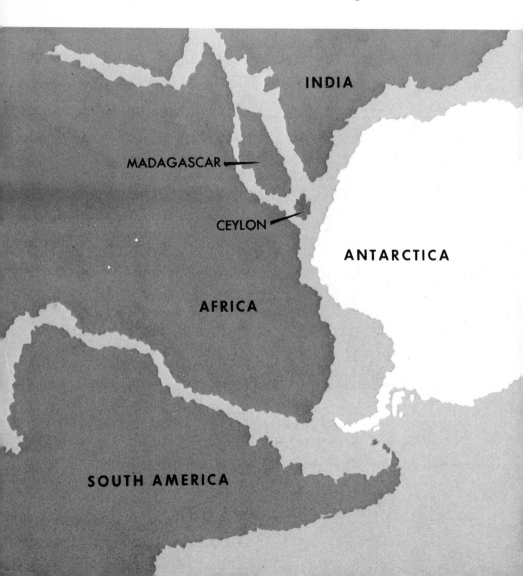

spin, is the Pole. If you could watch the earth long enough and carefully enough, you would notice that our globe wobbles slightly as it rotates. Just a little, but enough so that the one point which isn't spinning (the Pole) wouldn't always remain directly below you. In the course of a year, you would see it move in a series of lazy ovals 50 or 60 feet in diameter. Over the course of ten years you might even see the *center* of those ovals shift by as much as five feet. This doesn't seem like much of a move, but the age of the earth is measured in hundreds of millions of years. During all that time the Poles may have wandered considerably.

AUSTRALIA

NEW ZEALAND

Map shows how Antarctica, South America, Australia, Africa and India might have fit together.

Chances are that the continents have done some traveling too. Many geologists now agree that Antarctica, South America, Australia, Africa and India were once joined together in a supercontinent which they call Gondwana. This would explain similarities in plants and minerals between places which are now separated by thousands of miles of ocean. It would also solve a puzzle raised by magnetism in Australian and Antarctic rocks:

Rocks may become slightly magnetic as they are being formed; for example, as molten lava from a volcano cools down. This makes them almost like signposts, pointing to the magnetic poles at that particular moment. Later, the magnetic poles themselves may shift; but the rock-magnets won't budge. By comparing the "compasses" in several rocks of the same age, you should be able to tell where they were in relation to each other when they were formed. Using this method, it seems certain that the area of Antarctica called Wilkes Land was once nestled right up next to Australia.

The giant continent of Gondwana was probably centered in an area halfway between the South Pole and the equator. When it split up, most of the pieces drifted closer to the equator, but Antarctica was forced in the opposite direction. Eventually it became our single frozen continent.

The idea of "continental drift" was first suggested by a handful of scientists even before Scott and Amundsen carried out their expeditions. Both explorers, incidentally, were curious about the coal they saw in Antarctica. But many people poked fun at the drift theory then because they believed that the continents must be anchored firmly to a smooth earth crust, which formed the bottoms of the oceans. It was only much later that other geologists refined the proposal. Today, it is widely believed that continents are comparatively light in weight. They float on the

Three petrified logs in the Horlick Mountains show that there were once large trees near the center of Antarctica.

denser material of the ocean floor, whose creeping movements are caused by differences in temperature from one area to another. If this is so, Antarctica could easily have spent enough time in a temperature zone to build up dense vegetation. It appears that this happened about 250 million years ago, after Antarctica had already been covered once by an ice sheet in an earlier cold era.

Aside from its coal beds, Antarctica poses many other puzzles for geologists and geographers — the men who

Geologists camp near Mount Tyree, which towers nearly 17,000 feet above sea level in the Sentinel Range.

study the nature and shape of the earth. For quite a few years, scientists have argued about whether Antarctica is really a single, continuous continent or a group of large and small islands. There are some places far inland which lie below sea level. If all the snow and ice were removed from the Antarctic, would these areas become giant valleys or would they be arms of the ocean?

Studying the surface of a land buried under miles of snow is no easy matter. The usual method is to set off a small explosion under the snow and wait for the sound to echo off the rock below. The time it takes tells how deep the snow is. Recently, scientists have found that they can get faster results by using radar signals instead of sound waves; but this is still a relatively slow process, and it gives meager results for a continent which has only been crossed by a handful of ground parties so far.

Another way is to study magnetic changes from place to place. These changes are due partly to the thickness of the ground layer under the snow. To measure the changes, an instrument the size of a fire extinguisher is trailed along on a 100-foot line behind an airplane. But this system has its drawbacks, too, because other factors have an effect on the readings; and even an experienced geophysicist can't guarantee that his interpretations of the data are correct.

To make a long story short, the three-dimensional maps of Antarctica which exist today are based on three sources: 1) the position of those mountains which are tall enough to peek through the snow; 2) measurements along the narrow paths which traverses have covered; and 3) educated guesswork.

The rocks found in Antarctica have been dated by studying them with sensitive Geiger counters. The amount of natural radioactivity left in them indicates how long it has been since they crystallized. The older they are, the less radioactivity remains. These studies and others show that the Antarctic Peninsula appeared long after the rest of the continent. Its steep, jagged mountains look like a continuation of the Andes of South America, and they probably are.

Because the ground elevation drops sharply near the southern end of this peninsula, a number of persons have guessed that a valley below sea level might connect the Ross and Weddell ice shelves. This would mean that the famous peninsula was really a long, skinny island. In 1964, however, a careful survey showed that there is definitely a narrow strip of land connecting the peninsula with Eastern Antarctica.

Other evidence points to the existence of a solid continent under the central part of the ice cap. The Russians report that land underlies almost all of the snow in the remote inland regions where they maintain bases. At the South Pole station, U. S. seismologists (who "listen" constantly for earthquakes) agree. Shock waves don't travel as rapidly through an island group as they do through land, they say. Their seismographs at the Pole wouldn't record tremors as promptly as they do unless they were on a continent.

As troublesome as ice might be to some scientific studies in Antarctica, it is also the object of research itself. Snow accumulates gradually, in layers. It is possible to tell one year's layer from another, and experts can even detect a difference between the snow which fell during the winter and the snow which fell during the warmer summer. By measuring the thickness of each layer and studying the size of individual crystals, scientists in Antarctica can discover what the weather there was like hundreds of years ago. A deep pit in the snow is a calendar of the continent's history.

Weather isn't the only tale the snow pit can tell. When snow falls, it carries with it all sorts of bits suspended in the atmosphere — dust, plant spores, bacteria and volcanic ash. A typical project has been to use Antarctic snow to find out how quickly the insect killer DDT invaded the world's water supply after people first began to use it widely in the mid-1940's. Knowing the dates of famous volcanic eruptions helps to check the origin of certain snow layers. Otherwise some might be hard to distinguish because of the way they have been compressed by the

Snow cores are weighed.

enormous weight pressing down on them from above. Air pollution can be studied in the snow, too. Carbon dioxide shows industrial contamination; abnormal radioactivity measures fallout from nuclear explosions.

Drills have been built to bring up snow samples from far below the bottom of any ordinary snow pit. Usually the drill is hollow, with its cutting edge around the outside. A cylinder of snow is brought to the surface through the center of the drill itself. The latest models use heat instead of metal teeth to bite through the snow and ice, and these drills make it possible to study the ice right down to the bedrock of the Antarctic continent. Modern scientists believe that the ice and snow have completely covered Antarctica for about a million years. If they are right, we are bound to learn a great deal about the earth's history by getting to the bottom of the ice cap.

Is the world's climate getting milder? There is some

65

evidence that it has been for the last 100 years or so, and the snows of Antarctica seem to confirm this. If this is part of a long-range trend, the ice cap might gradually melt again. There is not much danger that it would disappear altogether, but we can imagine what a rise of just a few feet in the ocean level would mean to the world's great seaports. Think of Manhattan surrounded by dikes like the ones in Holland.

The ice shelves of Antarctica are always on the move. A picket fence of stakes driven into the icy surface or a cable dropped through the shelf to the sea bottom can be watched to show the direction and speed of the motion. One American scientist using such methods estimates that the Ross Ice Shelf pushes toward the open sea at the rate of several inches an hour.

Although an Antarctic ice shelf is attached to the continent, most of it projects over the ocean. It floats on the water, and it rises and falls in gentle, rhythmic waves. Sooner or later, a crack will appear and rip across its surface. With a rumble like a barrage of heavy artillery, a section of the ice shelf will split off or "calve." A new iceberg is born.

Glaciers, which move across land, can change the face of the continent. Ice looks solid, but its own weight can make it flow downhill like thick syrup. Just as a loose ice cube in your refrigerator will fasten itself to a carton or a piece of metal, so the glaciers will wrap themselves around rocks and other debris in their path. The moving sheet of ice can clear away sizable boulders, so that if it ever retreats it will leave a completely different landscape from the one it found originally.

Many of the surface features which are now exposed in Antarctica show the results of glacial action. But others are not explained so easily. The "dry valleys" near McMurdo Sound are one example.

66

A glacier in Taylor Valley

Unfrozen lakes in Antarctica
have puzzled visitors since the days of Scott.

These valleys are completely free of snow. They are several degrees warmer than the surrounding area; and their surface is rough and cracked, like alligator hide. There are lakes, too. Some are covered with ice, while others are quite open; and their depth ranges from a few inches to several hundred feet. The upper end of the Wright Valley is crisscrossed by channels up to a hundred yards wide, which divide into a checkerboard of rocky towers. To a geologist, these valleys are more than a mystery; they are many mysteries in one. Nobody can answer all the questions.

Volcanic action might explain the lakes. Mt. Erebus is only a few miles away, and you would expect to find underground hot springs in this neighborhood. Furthermore, the lakes are smaller than they used to be; you can still see the older shorelines. This means that the minerals dissolved in their water are more concentrated, and this lowers their freezing point.

Explaining the temperature in the dry valleys is like trying to say which came first — the chicken or the egg. Bare rock traps heat from the sun more easily than snow, whose glistening surface reflects the sun's rays. But how did the valley free itself of snow to begin with? Freakish winds are probably the answer.

"Patterned ground" comes from repeated freezing and thawing of the soil. But how explain the towering rock castles in Wright Valley? They look like the formations in eastern Washington State, which were created by floods. The rock castles of Antarctica are relatively new, because their surfaces have not yet been eroded much by the wind. Does that mean that this region was the scene of floods within the last few thousand years?

The Wright Glacier, which sticks its giant flat tongue into the head of the valley, could have acted like a dam. Water may have built up behind it until it spilled over like a giant waterfall, or even burst through the glacier itself, as a stream of liquid melts through an ice cube. But where did the water come from in this frozen desert? Once again, volcanoes may be the explanation. As recently as 1962, a South African supply ship which had been trapped in the Antarctic ice pack for over a week was freed by an underwater eruption. A subterranean volcano hundreds of miles away from the stranded ship churned up the ocean with such force that a 10-foot-thick ice crust cracked and splintered. Think of what might happen if lava, flame and hot ash spurted forth suddenly, right in the midst of an ice reservoir on the continent itself.

The men who trace the history of Antarctica face many mysteries, so they must use informed imagination to try to fill in the gaps. Even the finest scientific instruments don't guarantee accuracy, as shown by the disagreement between U. S. and British scientists over snow depth along the cross-continental route of Sir Vivian Fuchs. Sir Vivian's party estimated that the snow was between 8,000 and 9,000 feet in one area, but later checks by a U. S. group gave a reading of 3,000 feet deeper. Sharp differences like these hint that our ideas about Antarctica are probably in for more changes in the future.

Rock, fossils and ice are difficult books to read; but the Antarctic scientists are gradually learning the language. There is no doubt that the history is worth reading.

Some penguins lose their privacy in the interest of science.

CHAPTER FIVE

The Natives

I f there is anything at all which symbolizes Antarctica to most people, it is the penguin. Penguins
are funny to watch as they jostle against each other near
the edge of the ice. Dressed in the formal finery that
nature gave them, they look like little men at a party.

For the first one who slips or is nudged into the water,
however, the party may be ended quickly. Anxiously the
others will stop and peer over the side to watch what

happens. If a sharp-toothed leopard seal happens to be anywhere in the neighborhood, the poor penguin will soon become a sacrificial victim. Then his former play-mates may wander away to find a safer spot if they can. On the other hand, if his luck holds, this particular patch of water is presumably safe to use as a playground. The rest of the penguins join him.

The whole process seems cruel . . . but so is all life in Antarctica. Both on land and in the freezing waters around the continent, the fight for survival is waged against live enemies as well as against wind, cold and darkness.

During thousands of years, nature has given the "na-tives" of Antarctica some strange talents and habits. By studying them, man can learn a few tricks which might someday help him to get along in those same hostile sur-roundings.

In a way, the Antarctic cold is a blessing. A general rule of nature seems to be that living things — plants, birds, fish and land animals — age more slowly when the tem-perature is low. Not many different *kinds* of life have managed to adapt to the Antarctic. But those that do, live longer than their relatives in warmer climates. More dif-ferent generations of birds and animals — parents, chil-dren, grandchildren, great-grandchildren, and so on — remain alive at the same time. There may not be much variety in the life south of the Antarctic Circle, but there certainly are some big families.

Partly as a result of this, the Antarctic Ocean is the richest in the world. The other reason for its fertility is that the bottom waters of the sea around Antarctica are in constant motion. Minerals and organic fertilizer are always being brought up toward the surface. There they feed the sea plants — which nourish the shrimp, fish and whales.

Whales, of course, are not fish. Whales are mammals,

like men and mice. They breathe air, and will drown if forced to stay under water indefinitely. They are also warm-blooded. And, believe it or not, they have arms, hands and fingers — although disuse during millions of years of ocean dwelling has gradually made the hands useless to whales of today, except as flippers.

About a dozen different kinds of whales live in the Antarctic regions, but the most impressive by far is the blue whale. He is the largest creature ever to inhabit the earth — more than twice as big as the most enormous dinosaurs known. Like those giant reptiles of long ago, whales need the buoyancy of water to support their great weight. Not only would a large whale be unable to move on land; his ribs would almost certainly collapse under his load of fat, which may total more than 130 tons. The food-rich waters of the Antarctic Ocean are perfect for such a creature, which needs about 6,000 pounds of fresh nourishment each day.

Considering the size of his diet, the blue whale is actually a dainty eater. Having no teeth, he is content with a steady fare of small red shrimp, called "krill." A whale will swim along through a school of krill with his jaws wide apart, filling his mouth with food and seawater. Then he rolls his tongue forward, pressing the mouthful against a kind of natural "soup strainer" just inside his upper lip. The water is forced out, but the krill stay in — where he can gulp them down at his leisure.

The whale's strainer is called baleen or whalebone, but it isn't really bone. It is made of hundreds of rows of horny plates, hanging down from the roof of his mouth and fringed at the bottom into hairlike bristles. Some of the smaller whales have teeth instead of baleen, but even then the teeth are not used for chewing. All whales gulp their food down whole.

No matter how cold the water, the temperature inside

a whale's body is always around 92 degrees — not much cooler than that of a human being. Layer upon layer of thick, fatty blubber protects him from the chilly sea; and his only temperature problem comes occasionally from overheating. Whales are fast swimmers (even the big blue ones have been clocked at 15 to 20 miles an hour); and such strenuous exercise would build up body heat to a dangerous point if it were not for another gift of nature. The flippers on each side and the big, flabby flukes at the end of a whale's tail act like radiators to get rid of excess heat whenever necessary. This radiator system is controlled by a sort of thermostat; it is turned on and off by the way the whale's blood circulates.

A baby whale may be 20 to 25 feet long at birth, but it is relatively slim. Thus the youngsters are not as well shielded against extreme cold as their elders are. Prospective parents know this and will swim thousands of miles northward from the Antarctic so that their baby can be born in warmer water. Once his protective blubber has begun to build up, the whole family returns to the old feeding grounds — perhaps in the company of a hundred or more other whales.

Whales have excellent hearing, which they use like sonar in the dimly lighted ocean depths. They have voices ranging from a low, creaking groan to a high-pitched whistle; and they can spot a school of fish, an iceberg or an approaching enemy simply by giving off some sound and listening intently for its echo as it bounces off the object. A whale's cone-shaped ear plugs, incidentally, are a good key to his age. The plugs are built up at the rate of two layers each year.

In modern times the most dangerous foe of whales has been man. Just in the last 50 years, more than a million whales have been killed for their oil and other by-products. Whaling, which was one of man's first attractions to the Antarctic, is the area's only industry; and four out of every five catches today are made in the waters of the far South.

Shortly before World War II, whaling reached its peak with an annual catch of 45,000. Realizing that slaughter at this pace might bring a complete end to whales and whaling, the various interested nations agreed to limit the annual haul. Each country was given a definite quota. Mother whales and their babes were not to be hunted at all. The total annual quota is now about 10,000 blue whales or their equivalent — with a single blue whale being considered the equal of two fin whales, six sei whales, or one and a half humpbacks.

Efforts to preserve the Antarctic whales may be almost too late. Most countries have trouble catching the number of whales allowed each year, in spite of modern methods. Helicopters cruise ahead of motorized whalers, and man-made sonar tracks the prey under water. Noise-makers are used to frighten the whales, making them swim rapidly, get out of breath and surface more often so that they can be spotted. The plain, barbed harpoons of the early days have been replaced — first by explosive harpoons fired from deck guns, and more recently by barbed rods which electrocute the whale without spoiling any part of its carcass. Still, the annual catch dwindles.

Whales are smarter these days. No longer can the hunter ship expect a group (called a pod or a gam) to stick together while one whale after another is killed. The whales have learned at last to scatter in the face of such danger.

After a whale is killed, the body is pumped full of air to keep it afloat and marked with a red flag for pickup later on. Sometimes the whalers leave a radio transmitter or a radar reflector as a marker. Back at the factory ship, it will take less than an hour to remove and process the blubber, meat, bone, and liver from each catch.

Most whale oil — about half a million tons a year — is

The inflated carcasses of almost a dozen whales float alongside a "factory ship" in the Antarctic Ocean.

used now to make margarine and soap. The lean meat is sold as food, and it has become especially popular in Japan and Norway.

Among the other inhabitants of the Antarctic regions is one which is *called* a whale although it really isn't. A relative of the friendly dolphin, it has quite a different sort of reputation. It is a sleek 30-foot, black-and-white monster called the killer whale.

Each killer is armed with from 40 to 56 strong sharp teeth and a set of vicious instincts. He will hunt and kill seals and penguins, as well as even the largest of whales. Sometimes the killer does not even bother to eat his victims, being satisfied simply to destroy.

76

Searching for food or sport under the sea ice, a killer will swim about looking for telltale shadows. Having found one, he will dive to gather momentum and then hurl himself toward the surface, battering through two feet or more of ice to spill a helpless seal or penguin into the water — where a single bite can finish him off.

Packs of killer whales do not hesitate to attack one of the blimplike blue whales. Even the killers' powerful teeth cannot penetrate the thick hide of the blue giant, and they know that a blow from his thrashing flukes could be devastating, but they use a devilish kind of teamwork. Some of the killers will seize the flukes and hold them fast while others try to force their way into the blue's defenseless mouth. Their goal is the big soft tongue, which killer whales consider a delicacy. Once they have been successful, the poor blue will usually bleed to death.

Whalers claim the agile killers will sometimes follow their ships and even help them make a catch, realizing somehow that they can expect to be rewarded by several tons of tongue after the big whale has been brought alongside. Whalers have come to recognize individual killers — even giving them nicknames.

An Australian group reported once that killers attracted their attention on shore and actually led them to a pod of migrating humpback whales. When one of the humpbacks had been harpooned, two killers took turns flopping across his blowholes to block his breathing while two others swam under his head to keep him from diving. With such savage enemies, it is little wonder that whales sometimes shed great, waxy tears. Their life is not an easy one.

There have been several reports of killer whales attacking human beings. One such frightening account from Scott's journals is frequently quoted. But, so far as we know, no man has ever actually been harmed by one. The

Killer whales travel in packs.

men who were chased might have been mistaken for seals — which are everyday snacks for the killers. Seals are such favorites, in fact, that 32 of them were once found in the stomach of a single killer whale.

Some whales wander closer to the Antarctic continent than others, but of course none can venture too far under the thick, solid pack ice. The cavernous lungs of the larger whales permit them to remain under water and ice for well over an hour at a time, but eventually they must surface to breathe. This is when they produce the towering spouts which are seen so often in old whaling pictures. In spite of their appearance, the spouts are not streams of water; they are actually clouds of warm gas, condensing into droplets in the cold outside air.

There *is* life under the ice shelves, though. In fact, an icebreaker pounding its way through a heavy pack will sometimes turn up cakes of white ice smeared with what looks from a distance like gobs of peanut butter. This is algae — a living plant which can get energy from the sun even through 12 to 15 feet of ice. There are more vigorous forms of life under the ice, too — starfish and clams, sea spiders and sponges, squid and brightly colored jellyfish with tentacles 30 feet long.

Sea creatures taken from
the bottom of Waddell Sea, at a depth of almost 1,000 feet

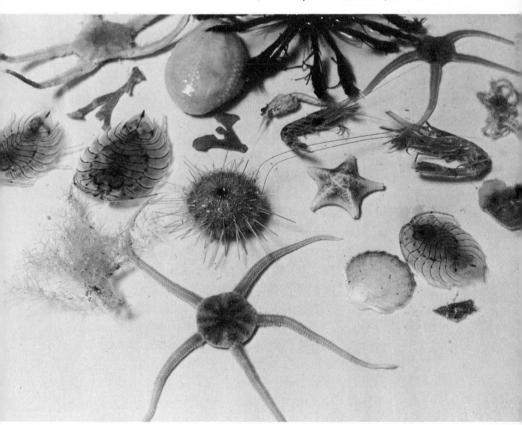

Weird fish populate the waters around Antarctica.

And there are fish — ugly ones, with heads like dragons, as well as more familiar-looking relatives of the cod and the perch. Fish up to five feet in length have been taken through the ice near McMurdo Sound, at the very edge of the Ross Ice Shelf.

The fish of the Antarctic Ocean are a strange lot. Some have colorless blood in their veins. Since so much oxygen is dissolved in the cold waters, perhaps the oxygen-processing red blood cells are unnecessary; but this wouldn't explain why all fish in the area haven't adapted themselves in the same way. The "ice fish" are a mystery.

Seals swim under the ice, too; but like whales they must come up for air. The Weddell seal and some others use their teeth to gnaw breathing holes in the sea ice. These seals are great divers; and biologists who strap depth gauges to some of these lazy-looking 700-pound fellows have found that they can descend more than a quarter of a mile beneath the surface. A Weddell seal may stay under water for half an hour at a time, frisking about in spite of pressure that would crush a human swimmer.

Another curiosity is that seals somehow avoid the "bends." A human diver always suffers these painful cramps if he rises to the surface too quickly. Nitrogen from the air is dissolved in his blood under pressure, and it turns into gas again if the pressure is reduced suddenly. Skin divers wish we could learn the seals' diving and breathing secrets, so they could try to copy them — just as long-distance swimmers have begun to imitate the effortless swimming style of seals.

Besides the Weddell, four other types of seals are found in Antarctica. The first you might see from a ship approaching the Antarctic is the smaller, white crabeater seal. He spends most of his time far out on the pack ice, and he doesn't hide his dislike of intruders. He will hiss and bare his teeth, but this ferociousness is just an act. His diet is a soft one like that of the blue whale; and the crabeater is less likely to be a hunter than the hunted — being another dinner favorite of the killer whale.

Many visitors to Antarctica never see the Ross seal at all, because that shy and solitary gentleman is very rare. Anyone who has been close to this "singing seal," however, is sure to remember his birdlike chirping.

The lumbering elephant seals live mostly on the islands north of Antarctica; but hundreds of them also come to the beaches of the continent itself each year to shed their fur and outer skins. The largest of these flabby creatures are more than 20 feet long and weigh about four tons, but the name "elephant" is not based only on size. The snout of a full-grown male may be 15 inches long, resembling an elephant's trunk when the seal fills it with air to trumpet a challenge.

The last of the Antarctic seals is one to avoid if possible

81

— the speedy, spotted sea leopard. His needle-sharp teeth are feared even by other seals, for the leopard sometimes turns cannibal. Furthermore, frightened explorers have found that it takes a high-powered rifle to stop the fierce charges of a leopard seal across the ice.

A seal cannot crawl on all fours, since its flippers are chiefly adapted to swimming. But its long, streamlined body can wriggle almost like a snake's; and the leopard especially can glide rapidly over a smooth surface.

Nevertheless, seals spend most of their lives in the water. The ocean offers them food. It keeps them warm, too. The water temperature is just above the freezing point, even though air above it may be 60 degrees below zero. A baby seal will take to the water when he is only about three weeks old. The babies grow quickly, doubling their birth weight within a couple of weeks and quintupling it before they are two months old.

Weddell seals (a mother
and her pup) are not a bit frightened by the photographer.

Although seals do not ordinarily travel very far inland, their bodies have been found as far as 35 miles from the coast, in an area 3,000 feet above sea level. The mystery is how and why they got there. Scientists can tell that these particular remains are thousands of years old, and that the seals apparently starved to death; but they can only guess at the rest of the story. Perhaps these seals were trapped ashore by an early freeze and driven inland in a vain search for food.

Overland travel is quite a different story to Antarctica's mascot, the penguin. He likes the water too, but has been known to travel hundreds of miles across the ice. Penguins are magnificent polar "navigators," and one test group found its way home over a 2,400-mile route.

Not all penguins look alike, by a long shot. There are 17 different recognized species, including some with flecks of bright orange plumage. Only five kinds live in Antarctica, however, and three of these (the chinstrap, gentoo and macaroni penguins) are limited to the Antarctic Peninsula and Antarctic islands. Without a doubt, the living symbols of Antarctica are the other two — the comical little Adélie and the solemn emperor.

Adélies stand about 15 inches high and weigh 10 to 15 pounds. The hulking emperors are about three times as tall, and may weigh up to 75 or 80 pounds. But ancient fossils found in Antarctica show that both varieties once had a big brother — a five-foot penguin which may have weighed 250 pounds.

It seems strange, but the friendly little penguin appears to be a fairly direct descendant of the dinosaurs of old. Some of the reptiles evolved into birds, while others became land or sea residents. The penguin, with stunted wings and scaly feathers, doesn't seem to belong completely to land, sea or air.

Penguins are graceful swimmers, and then can whisk through the water at the speed of a motorboat. Sometimes a group of Adélies will even put on a regular water ballet. They will skim across the surface, dive deep, then leap out of the water like porpoises, only to repeat the routine. Their nests are on land, though, so the climax always comes at the edge of the ice. From an underwater swimming start, 20 to 30 feet offshore, the penguins will finally head toward the ice and leap up at the last moment. Hurtling six or seven feet into the air, wings at their sides, the birds will land feet first and shuffle away — the performance over.

If you have ever seen the circus clowns who flop around in oversized shoes, you can picture a penguin's walk. No wonder a penguin doesn't always bother with such a clumsy means of propulsion. When he is on ice and in a real hurry, he simply flops down on his stomach and uses his flipper-wings to push himself over the smooth surface. A penguin can scoot along this way about as fast as a man can trot.

The Adélie penguin's sense of direction seems to be related in some way to the sun. If he is released in a strange part of the continent he will head due north, toward the coast. That is, he will do this if the sun is shining. Penguins become confused when the sky is overcast, just as they do if one of the biologists has subjected them to alternate periods of bright light and darkness before turning them loose. One thing is reasonably certain; penguin's built-in compass has nothing to do with magnetism. Birds released near the South Magnetic Pole find their way to the coast as quickly as any of the others.

After a penguin reaches the coast, he seems to find his way back to his home base by means of landmarks. And experiments with tape recordings show that once he reaches the rookery (nesting area), he will be able to recognize his own family by the rough, low-pitched, squawking sounds of their voices.

Like other native Antarcticans, penguins have been well fitted for life there. The lack of fresh water on their fishing trips doesn't bother them at all; they can drink salt water from the sea and eat krill (which is just as salty as sea water), eliminating the salt in some fashion through glands just above their eyes. Cold is no problem either, thanks to their layers of fat. Emperors, in fact, seem to thrive on the low temperatures. They go south for the winter, which in the Southern Hemisphere means heading right into the frigid blackness of continuous night.

Emperor penguins lay their eggs in the dead of winter, and so begins the most difficult baby-sitting job on earth. Unlike the Adélies, who build small nests of pebbles which they have collected or pilfered from each other, the emperor and his mate have no real home at all. Almost as soon as the single egg is laid, the mother penguin places it carefully on the father's webbed feet; and he covers it with the thick furry folds of his tummy. This natural

An Adélie penguin is unwrapped
and turned loose in an experiment to test homing instincts.

"potbellied stove" will keep the egg warm despite temperatures below zero; and for two whole months the patient papa will remain in this position without food, moving about only to avoid drifting snow (which he may nibble to satisfy his thirst). Luckily the bottoms of the emperor's feet are covered with thick callouses which reduce contact with the frigid ground. At times, though, it still becomes so unbearably cold that the bird will rock back on his heels, always careful to protect the egg nestled on his insteps.

Emperor penguin and chick

When the bitter winds begin to blow, hundreds of members of this Antarctic Fathers' Club will huddle together for warmth and protection; but the going is rough. And woe to the biologist who has to disturb the group on a wintry scientific egg hunt. The powerful flipper of an adult emperor can break a man's arm.

Where has mama gone all this time? Off to the northern edge of the fast ice, across miles of freshly frozen sea ice, collecting groceries. There is no food at all on the continent during the winter; but by the time she returns, the precious egg — big as a man's fist — will be ready to hatch into a fuzzy, helpless and hungry chick. The mother penguin, who has been gorging herself with krill, fish and squid, will bring up food from her own stomach to nourish the baby. It may not sound very appetizing to us humans, but baby penguins think this system is just fine. Papa is happy too, of course, because the return of his mate means that he can head north to break his fast also.

There are many other birds in and around the Antarctic — petrel, albatrosses, skuas. The Russians have reported one area where the bird population is the equivalent of 50,000 per square mile. Yet an invisible wall bars some species as effectively as a wire cage. North of Antarctica lies an irregular belt line, 25 to 30 miles wide, where the cold waters from the south meet the warmer currents of the Atlantic, Pacific and Indian oceans. In some places it is only a few hundred miles from the continent, while in other areas the distance may be over a thousand miles. North of this belt — called the Antarctic Convergence — live a vast number of seabirds who simply refuse to cross it. If you see a bird venture into this area at sea, you can bet that he is a real Antarctican.

To the true polar dweller, the Convergence is no barrier in either direction. Birds banded by scientists in Antarctica have been sighted frequently in Africa, Australia

Mother skua guards her chick.

and South America. In fact, one variety (the little Arctic tern) spends six months of every year near the North Pole and the other six months amid the Antarctic pack-ice. In this way, he manages to live in almost perpetual daylight.

Antarctic birds come in all sizes — from petrels no bigger than sparrows to several varieties of albatross whose wingspan may be eight to 12 feet. Some stay close to the ice pack, while others trail ships. In general they are good fishermen and beautiful to watch as they soar gracefully over the waves, swooping down only once in a while to pick up a quick snack.

The skua has provoked many an argument among old Antarctic hands. Most call him a vulture, but a stubborn few compare him to the eagle. His habits are untidy, and he raids penguin rookeries for eggs and chicks. But his defenders argue that this helps the penguin population in the long run by weeding out the weaklings and keeping it in line with the food supply. At any rate, there is no doubt that the skua is the most daring explorer among all Antarctic birds. Skuas have been spotted in the sky within a few miles of the South Pole itself.

Aside from the birds, the seals and the fish, one might suppose that Antarctica is completely devoid of native life. This is certainly true by ordinary standards. There are no polar bears or pack wolves, no rodents or reindeer. It is not nearly as easy a place as the Arctic in which to survive. But this is the very reason why visiting scientists look harder at what *is* there. They usually consider the plants and insects — even the microbes — as a scientifically important part of the Antarctic population.

By this definition, Antarctica is inhabited by a number of "land animals"; but they are pretty puny ones. The largest is a wingless fly about a quarter of an inch long.

Tiny marine creatures are examined in the biology laboratory at McMurdo Station.

Some other insects, called springtails or snow fleas — as well as eight-legged mites — are also found, usually under rocks. Naturally, they have no fur or blubber to keep them warm; but their bodies do produce a substance called glycerol. This is very much like the antifreeze used in automobiles and it works the same way. It keeps the insects from turning to ice.

In spite of this handy habit, an insect may live through many "seasons" in a single summer. An Antarctic rock can be a pretty comfortable spot in the summertime. Regardless of the air temperature, the constant sunshine may bake its surface to a high of 85 degrees or so. But if a storm should come up, the temperature plummets. When this happens, the insects relax in a deep sleep. In a way, they "hibernate" — like bears in the wintertime. When the rock heats up again — hours later or months later — the tiny creatures are as good as new.

Flies and insects bring up the question of disease . . . and the old story that there are no germs in Antarctica. Nonsense! The continent may be as white as the inside of an operating room; but there are plenty of bacteria. Yeast and other bacteria even grow in the otherwise lifeless lakes of Antarctica, including the salty ones. They have also been found in the snow and ice itself. Ninety feet below the surface of the South Pole, microbiologists uncovered some germs which appeared to have been trapped there at least a century ago. Using face masks and sterilized instruments, they were careful to avoid mixing modern bacteria with these 19th-century relics. If their technique was successful (and they were not simply collecting specimens which had been brought there recently by man), their results are surprising. *Staphylococcus* — an infection which was not even recognized by doctors until World War II — existed in the neighborhood of the South Pole in 1860. Furthermore the microbes in

Heat from electric bulbs drives Antarctic insects out of soil samples and down into a collections box. Below, an enlargement of the hardy little creatures.

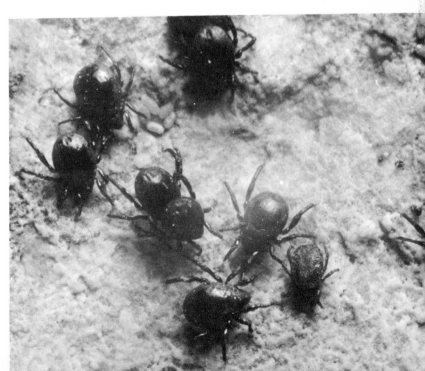

the ice were not dead, but revived in the laboratory when heated. Other frozen bacteria have been found closer to the coast; and these also have been "brought to life"; but in this case they were in the debris of abandoned camps and it is obvious that the fifty-year-old germs were brought to the Antarctic by early explorers.

The plants in Antarctica are old, too. At least, some of them are. The orange lichens there grow so slowly that some of the specimens which have been found must be about as old as the giant redwoods in California. Yet the biggest ones measure only a few inches across.

Lichens and moss are found almost any place in Antarctica where there is snow-free rock. Like the insects, these plants take advantage of solar heat. Algae are even less finicky. They grow in the snow itself, tinting it red, yellow or green, depending on the variety of algae. The primitive plants which grow on the bottomside of the sea ice are the hardiest of all. They have become so accustomed to their surroundings that they cannot survive if the temperature goes much above the freezing point.

Sometimes algae on the surface of damp rock seen from a distance will give the appearance of a well-kept lawn, but the only real grass which grows naturally in Antarctica is sparse and scraggly. There are two types of grass which bloom, but of course they grow only in the Antarctic Peninsula. That is the only part of the continent which is warm enough to provide a decent growing season; and — even more important — it is the *only* place where there is some rain every year.

A little relative of the pink — actually a low-growing herb — is the only other flowering plant which may be native to the Antarctic. Still, it could be that the flowering pink holds a forged passport. Many biologists believe that this plant was introduced accidentally by the early explorers. Some think the grasses got there the same way.

Meager as it is, the plant and animal life of the Antarctic is particularly fascinating; and scientists study it in almost every way imaginable. Seals are milked and have their throats swabbed. White seabirds are stained pink for easy identification. Fish are brought indoors and studied in glass aquariums. Penguins have numbers painted on their "shirt fronts." Miniature thermometers and radio transmitters are slipped inside bird eggs. Planes flying back and forth across the continent carry bug catchers in the hope of netting some new variety of insect. Every living thing which can be found is photographed, recorded, catalogued, and cross-referenced.

The natives are no longer alone.

This radio transmitter disguised
as an egg will check a penguin's nesting temperature.

CHAPTER SIX

Many Flags, No Borders

In October, 1958, many people were worried that a war might begin between the Communist world and the West over the island of Quemoy in the far Pacific. Within a few weeks, Premier Khrushchev was to threaten a second Berlin blockade. But in Antarctica, American Rear Admiral George J. Dufek got a friendly — almost casual — radio message from the Russian base at Mirnyy:

"We are planning a long new expedition, and we would

94

Australia's Mawson Station
on the Indian Ocean coast of Antarctica

like to take a look at the route by air. Would you mind if we landed at McMurdo Sound? And, by the way, could we borrow 1,500 gallons of aviation gasoline for the return flight?"

Admiral Dufek assured his "neighbors" on the other side of the continent that they would be welcome; and eight Russians soon made the 2,140-mile flight in a twin-engine Ilyushin IL-12 (which looks like an American

95

DC-3). On the way, they used the South Pole station as a checkpoint, wagging their red-starred wings in greeting to the American scientists below.

The practice of swapping scientists between the bases of different nations had been going on for several years, and a Soviet meteorologist named Astapenko happened to be at McMurdo Sound at the time. He printed the Russian words FOLLOW ME on a sign for the jeep at the airstrip, making it easier for the ground crew to direct the plane after it had touched down.

That night, Dr. Eugene Tolstikov and the other Russian visitors talked mostly about cooperation in Antarctic research. In spite of the low temperature outside, the Cold War seemed very far away.

The International Geophysical Year, of course, had made this kind of friendly exchange fairly common. During the 18-month period from July 1, 1957, to December 31, 1958, scientists all over the world had agreed to make special measurements and explorations at the same time. By putting all of their new information together in a worldwide pattern, they all hoped to learn more of the secrets of nature than they could ever discover one-by-one.

In the case of Antarctica, the spirit of the IGY led to the signing of a formal treaty which is scheduled to last at least until 1989. Peaceful cooperation is promised by 12 nations, including the United States and the Soviet Union.

The other countries which agreed to the treaty are Argentina, Australia, Belgium, Chile, France, Japan, New Zealand, Norway, the Union of South Africa and the United Kingdom. Each one has helped to explore the Antarctic, and most of them occupy one or more of the 30-odd bases there today. If the original signers agree unanimously, other countries can join the agreement also.

The Antarctic Treaty is not a very long one, but its rules are clear:

1) It covers every place on the globe south of the 60th meridian of South Latitude, not including the high seas but including ice shelves. The whole area is to be used only for peaceful purposes.

2) Weapons testing, military maneuvers and military bases are forbidden (although equipment and members of a nation's armed forces may provide transportation and support for scientific operations).

3) All countries agree to exchange the results of their scientific studies . . . and even to announce plans for any new ones. In fact, the other countries must be notified in advance whenever a new expedition is to be sent to Antarctica or when the groups there are to be shifted around.

4) Nuclear explosions are prohibited, and radioactive waste material from any source may not be dumped.

5) Any nation is free to check on the others at any time. They may fly over each other's bases or send inspection teams. Such visitors are even entitled to examine the equipment being used — including the ships and planes at Antarctic bases.

6) No country is required to give up the claims it now makes to any section of Antarctic territory, but no new claims will be made. Discoveries made while the treaty is in force will not be considered a legal support for future claims either.

Good timing may have been helpful in reaching this agreement. In 1948 the United States had suggested a "peace conference" among the seven nations which then claimed territory in Antarctica; but at that time the Russians protested. The Soviet Union had made no formal claims, but refused to be left out and announced that it would not respect any decisions reached by the conference. So that plan was dropped. Almost 10 years later, British Prime Minister Harold R. Macmillan suggested flatly that the continent be "internationalized," with each

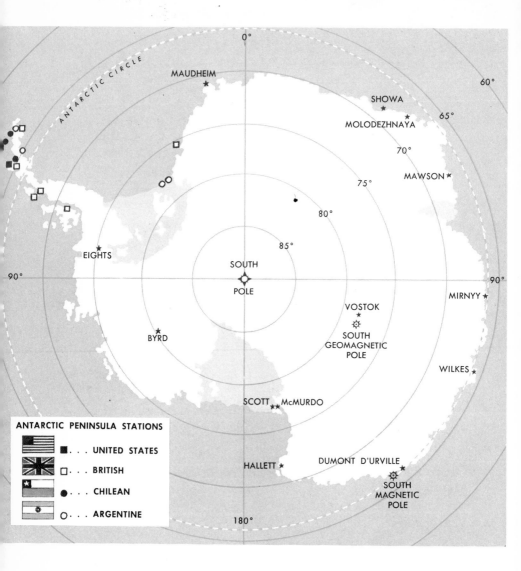

ANTARCTIC CIRCLE

0°

MAUDHEIM ★

60°

SHOWA ★

MOLODEZHNAYA ★

65°

70°

MAWSON ✳

75°

80°

85°

EIGHTS ★

SOUTH POLE ✦

90°

90°

MIRNYY ★

VOSTOK ★

BYRD ★

SOUTH GEOMAGNETIC POLE ☼

WILKES ★

SCOTT ★★ McMURDO

ANTARCTIC PENINSULA STATIONS

■ . . . UNITED STATES

□ . . . BRITISH

● . . . CHILEAN

○ . . . ARGENTINE

HALLETT ★

DUMONT D'URVILLE ★

SOUTH MAGNETIC POLE ☼

180°

nation giving up its territory. But Chile and Argentina didn't like that idea at all.

When President Eisenhower proposed a *limited* treaty on May 2, 1958, however, everyone finally seemed ready for the move. The IGY was more than half over, and it was proving to be a great success. At the same time, the sudden new activity of the Russians had frightened some countries into thinking that missile bases might be built near the Pole; and everybody wanted to prevent this from happening. Furthermore, countries in the Southern Hemisphere were afraid that large-scale nuclear bomb tests might be held in the Antarctic. This could spoil scientific research there, and dangerous radioactive fallout might be carried northward by the violent winds which originate in the Antarctic. Some agreement obviously had to be made quickly.

The treaty was signed late in 1959, suddenly guaranteeing that Antarctica would be the most peaceful spot on earth. Now that people have got used to the idea, this seems quite natural. It doesn't seem strange that scientists and explorers of various nationalities and philosophies should be willing to work together — especially in a place where all face the same hardships. In fact, the idea for the International Geophysical Year had come from the fact that nations had banded together earlier — in 1882-83 and again in 1932-33 — to study the region of the North Pole.

Nevertheless, Antarctica had had its share of international squabbles. Hitler, for example, considered the area in his plan for world conquest. During the 1938-39 polar season he sent an expedition commanded by Captain Alfred Ritscher to the coast due south of South Africa. Daily for three weeks, two seaplanes were catapulted from the deck of the German ship *Schwabenland,* with orders to fly back and forth across the territory which Norwegian explorers had named Queen Maud Land. The Germans made a far more thorough aerial study than Norway had done, finding vast regions which were surprisingly free of ice. Their planes covered 230,000 square miles in all, photographing almost half of this area. They also dropped several thousand metal poles, each marked with the swastika and pointed at the heavy tip so that the rod would dig into the ice and remain upright. This job done, the methodical German crew renamed the whole territory New Schwabenland . . . and claimed it as part of Hitler's Third Reich.

The simple matter of conflicting claims was not new or surprising. But Nazi Germany had more in mind than just changing names on the great white open spaces of the Antarctic map. Two years later, a couple of large Norwegian whaling ships — actually seagoing processing plants — were seized by boarding parties from the German raider *Pinguin* as they rested at anchor north of Queen Maud Land. Within hours, a supply ship and most of the nearby whaling convoy had been lured into the German trap; and the naval war in Antarctica was well under way.

The most important German base for these operations was not in Antarctica itself, but about 1,300 miles north — on the French-claimed island of Kerguelen. Halfway between Australia and Africa, this remote and glacier-

The Union of South Africa operates these snow tractors along the coast of Queen Maud Land, which Norway allows it to occupy.

capped island had been known chiefly for the tasty native cabbage it provided occasional visitors. Now, however, an Australian warship planted a different sort of crop in the waters around it — explosive mines aimed at discouraging the Nazi marauders.

In May, 1941, the HMS *Cornwall* located and sank the *Pinguin,* but not before she had captured a string of Allied merchant ships totaling more than 135,000 tons. Her sister ships *Atlantis* and *Komet* continued to prowl the southern seas.

Farther to the west, the British were afraid that the Germans might get help from Argentina in establishing naval bases on the Antarctic continent itself. The Argentines were neutral, but they had built up a large trade with Germany and many of their leaders were friendly to the Axis powers.

To defend themselves, the British decided to occupy the northernmost peninsula of Antarctica themselves. Secretly they sent a small party which reached Deception Island but could get no farther at first because of unusually thick ice and punishing storms. During the last year of World War II, the British stations provided regular weather reports to Allied ships; and since then they have been the headquarters of other scientific studies as well.

This section of Antarctica, which normally has the mildest climate and which is probably the most thoroughly explored, has been a consistent trouble spot. Here is why:

1) The British have claimed the peninsula — which they call Graham Land — since 1908 as a part of their colony in the Falkland Islands. In 1961 they converted the whole "Falkland Island Dependencies" into a separate colony and rechristened it British Antarctica.

101

2) Argentina says that the peninsula — San Martin Land — is really an extension of its own territory in the direction of the South Pole. And the Argentinians add that the Falkland Islands should belong to them, too.

3) Chile, like Argentina, bases its claim to the peninsula partly on a decree by Pope Alexander VI in 1493 — which settled a quarrel between Spain and Portugal by dividing the territories of the New World stretching "from pole to pole." Incidentally, the Chileans call the place O'Higgins Land (after their national hero, Bernardo O'Higgins).

For many years the United States referred to this sector of Antarctica as the Palmer Peninsula (so named for the young American sea captain mentioned in Chapter 2). Now, however, a compromise suggestion may wipe the slate clean. The disputed area will be listed in many new atlases as the Antarctic Peninsula. Perhaps this name will satisfy everybody.

At times the jealousy of rival countries over their claims in Antarctica has seemed a bit comical. At other times, however, it has seemed almost serious enough to cause bloodshed.

The port of Deception Island was used by American sealers from the time of their first voyages. Yet when the British visited the abandoned station in 1943 to search for German raiders they seemed terribly upset to find a bronze tablet which had been installed the previous year by the Argentine ship *Primero de Mayo*. Their major concern was probably over the fact that the tablet had used this convenient spot to stake a claim to roughly half a million squares miles of Antarctic territory. At any rate, the British removed the tablet, hoisted their flag, and posted their own claim. A year later, on their return voyage, they found the Argentine ship had come again. This time the announcement by the United Kingdom had been replaced by a painting of the Argentine flag — for which the loyal British sailors promptly substituted a painting of the Union Jack. And so on.

Actually, rocky little Deception Island hardly looks as if it is worth fighting over. It has relatively little ice and snow, but no grass or other vegetation either. In fact, it is nothing more than the cone of an extinct volcano, with one side blown out by some ancient explosion. The unpleasant odor of sulfur hangs over the place; and the gloomy black ring around the nine-mile-wide crater is decorated with crumbling ruins and an old, well-filled cemetery. In January, 1930, the bottom literally dropped out of this uninviting island. A violent earthquake lowered the bottom of the harbor by about 15 feet, clouds of steam rose from the water, and paint was blistered from the keels of ships at anchor there. Nevertheless, the seesaw struggle for sovereignty continued.

In 1948, Argentina sent 15 naval vessels along with its scientific and supply ships to Antarctica. Among other things, they went through the familiar ritual of changing several place names. The British reacted immediately. They sent a cruiser and a small frigate of their own into the same waters, but luckily the two forces did not meet. After this close call, Britain, Chile and Argentina agreed to avoid further incidents by banning naval maneuvers in the vicinity of Antarctica.

Four years later, however, a British landing party at nearby Hope Bay was fired on by Argentine forces, who arrested and deported them briefly. An apology was made quickly by the Argentine government, and the British returned peacefully. Since then, there have been no more such clashes. Argentina has refused the British suggestion that their conflicting claims be referred to the International Court of Justice, but hopefully the Antarctic Treaty will keep the problem from flaring up again.

This Is Antarctica

National claims to the Antarctic are based on many factors. Discovery is one, and exploration is another. Using a slightly different approach, Chile reminds others that she is the country closest to the Antarctic continent; and Argentina points out that her citizens have occupied Antarctic territory (Laurie Island) continuously for more than 60 years. The British sent magistrates to Deception Island every summer for 20 years to bolster their claim by showing that British law was being enforced there.

And, of course, there are postage stamps:

The territorial claims of Australia, Argentina, Chile, New Zealand and Norway are shown in the stamps they have issued.

Britain, Australia, France and New Zealand regularly issue stamps to be used in and by their "Antarctic Territories." Other countries at least operate post offices (with distinctive postmarks) for their Antarctic bases. And virtually all countries which have been active there issue commemorative stamps which remind the world of their interest and achievements.

A favorite bit of propaganda is to include on such stamps a map of Antarctica, showing the area claimed by the issuing country. The typical claim is a wedge-shaped slice. It will start along the coast, where landings or explorations have been made, and cut into the continent as if it were a pie with the South Pole at its center.

One exception (in shape, at least) is the French claim, which is not limited to the Adélie Coast. In 1955 France announced that its Antarctic triangle would be lumped with the Kerguelen, Crozet, Saint Paul and Amsterdam islands in the South Indian Ocean, and that the whole lot would be granted "home rule" as a single territory. The 100 or so Frenchmen, 2,000 head of wild cattle, numerous elephant seals and more than one million penguins who populate these "Southern and Antarctic French Lands" now have their own budget as well as their own postage stamps. They are represented in Paris by a Consultative Council attached to the Overseas Ministry.

The United States and the Soviet Union agreed on one major point about the Antarctic long before the treaty was signed. Neither makes any specific territorial claims; and neither recognizes the claims made by anyone else. As early as 1924, the American State Department announced that it would not recognize discovery alone as a legal claim to new territory "unless the discovery was followed by actual settlement of the discovered country." The word "settlement" was not defined, but it has been

New Zealand's Scott Base is so close to McMurdo Station that it gets frequent friendly visits from U. S. scientists and support forces.

fairly clear that the United States prefers to keep the whole question open.

Most countries interested in the Antarctic still take an occasional opportunity to "wave the flag." Official visitors to the Antarctic "possessions" have included all sorts of high government dignitaries — even the presidents of Chile and Argentina, and Prince Philip of Great Britain.

Despite the official policy of the United States, American explorers have usually posted notices of their pioneering visits. And when a group of U. S. surveyors near Wilkes Station found a vodka bottle containing a Russian claim to discovery of the area, they returned the marker to its resting place in a cairn of rocks — but only after adding a map of the sector published in the United States *before* the Russian visit. Just a polite reminder that the Stars and Stripes had been there first.

The men of many nations have helped open Antarctica to the world. The first to reach the Pole was a Norwegian; the first group to spend a winter in the Antarctic were Belgians. A Frenchman, J. S. C. Dumont d'Urville, made the first landing on the Atlantic side of the continent; and the first expedition to cross Antarctica on the ground represented the British Commonwealth. Major aerial surveys have been carried out by the United States and the Soviet Union, and rugged teams from both countries have built permanent bases deep in the interior.

In general, all of the nations have been happy to work together. Twice the United States has even transferred the custody of bases which it was no longer using to other countries — Wilkes Station to Australia and Ellsworth Station to Argentina. The Russians allowed Polish explorers to use their Oasis Station, which is on the coast near Wilkes. New Zealand and the United States operate Hallett Station jointly. And the South Africans, who had no base of their own, have been allowed to occupy Norway's station in Queen Maud Land.

The Soviet Union's Mirnyy Station

The present treaty seems to be working smoothly. Late in 1963, Australia, New Zealand and the United Kingdom sent the first formal inspection teams to the various United States stations; and the United States named inspectors for other countries' bases — including the Russians' Mirnyy and Vostok stations. The visits were completely cordial, and — as everybody expected — it was obvious that the treaty terms were being observed.

During the International Years of the Quiet Sun (1964-65) the American and Russian scientists cooperated in a study of cosmic rays. These rays are actually bits of atoms which come to the earth from the sun and from distant parts of the universe. The earth acts like a magnet which traps most of the incoming cosmic particles in giant belts, which come to a point at each pole. By erecting tall radio antennas at three U.S. bases, a British and a Russian station, the scientists could bounce signals to each other off the roof of the earth's atmosphere — a layer called the ionosphere. Cosmic rays reinforce this layer, causing more of the radio waves to spring back toward earth. By measuring the strength of the signals continuously, the men were able to tell how strong the cosmic bombardment was during the periods when the sun was "quiet" — relatively free from electrical storms on its own surface. Thus, even while the world's two greatest powers were competing in a spectacular space race, their representatives in Antarctica could help each other in studies which might assist both in their journeys to the moon and beyond.

In Antarctica itself, the simple rules of the treaty have been expanded by special agreements among all 12 parties:

Weather information collected anywhere in the Antarctic is radioed to Australia, where it is put together as a basis for daily forecasts. These are broadcast back to the entire continent. Some radio frequencies are set aside especially for emergency use; and it almost goes without saying that a plane crash, medical problem or ground accident will automatically bring help from the nearest station, regardless of nationality.

Historical sites are to be preserved, the 12 nations have agreed. Never again will one nation tear down the earlier buildings of another, just to remove evidence of settlement — as has happened on the disputed Antarctic Peninsula.

The meager wildlife of Antarctica is now about as well protected as the animals in a national park. Dogs are no longer permitted to run free. Explosives and firearms may not be used near the places where seals or birds are breeding; and aircraft are also warned to avoid low flights over these areas. Even people on foot are instructed by international agreement not to disturb the colonies persistently or unnecessarily. Furthermore, ships are warned not to dump oil in such a way that it might injure the wildlife.

Technically, Antarctic explorers are even warned to "keep off the grass." Native plants are not to be destroyed or injured, except in the gathering of scientific specimens. Plants brought in from other parts of the world must be grown under controlled conditions, so that they will not spread. If the plants reproduced too widely, they might upset the natural balance or even fool scientists into believing that some had originated in Antarctica.

Antarctica today is like a clean, bright test tube. Or one might call it a whole, vast outdoor laboratory. The talents of every race and many nations are assembled there. Free of worries about international politics, they can come and go as they like. This is an atmosphere in which — despite the stubborn resistance of nature — we are bound to make rapid progress.

CHAPTER SEVEN

The Antarctic Airline

M ost Americans who travel to Antarctica these days go there by air. But timetables don't mean much on the Antarctic Airline. The men who gather in one corner of an airport in New Zealand awaiting a flight know they can't leave for "the ice" unless conditions are just right. Perhaps they waited there yesterday, only to have the trip delayed by a report of bad weather at their destination. Or maybe they even started the journey, but had to turn back because of 80-mile-an-hour headwinds and storms which nobody could have predicted. So they will sit there patiently amid their duffle bags, drinking coffee from a vending machine and talking about the flight with those who have made it before.

It is 2,200 miles from Harewood International Airport in Christchurch, New Zealand, to the smooth patch of ice which is the main landing strip for McMurdo Station, Antarctica. More than 90 percent of the distance is across water and ice, through the worst latitudes imaginable —

Aircraft stand out sharply against the ice at McMurdo.

the Furious Fifties and the Screaming Sixties. The only radio station between the tip of New Zealand's South Island and Antarctica is on a U. S. picket ship near the midway point. Crossing the Antarctic Ocean is like flying from New York to Denver, knowing only what the weather is like at Springfield, Illinois.

Each of the Navy and Air Force pilots who have volunteered to fly this route knows what an emergency landing in the icy ocean would mean. Even if the plane survived its impact on the choppy surface and stayed afloat long enough for its passengers to escape, their chances of rescue would be dim. In a rubberized survival suit, a man might last about an hour in those waters. Without such protection he would die in minutes from exposure. The solution of the men who run the airline is simple:

"Play it safe. Don't take chances. It's better to be listed as late in the logbook than to show up as a casualty in the newspapers."

A flight to McMurdo aboard a big C-124 Globemaster is unlike any other airline trip in the world. Passengers disappear into the gaping mouth of the plane like fish being swallowed by a whale. Inside, the steel ribs seem to pulsate in the dim light; and an enormous steel tongue splits the belly of the monster into an upper and a lower deck.

For takeoff, the 60 or 70 passengers line the narrow benches along either side of the plane. Once in the air, they are free to unfasten their safety belts and wander about. The windows are small; and for a while there is little to see anyway. Some of the men stretch out on the metal decks or on the crates which fill the forward end of the ship. A nap 5,000 feet above the wild blue ocean somehow seems perfectly natural . . . for the flight will take about half a day, and they will want to be wide awake later on.

During the trip the plane's heaters are gradually turned

A turboprop Army helicopter is loaded
aboard an Air Force C-124 for delivery to Antarctica.

off, and before too long the cabin temperature will be near the freezing point. Passengers are advised to put on their specially issued clothing one layer at a time, staying comfortable yet becoming accustomed to the cold. It may have been a lovely spring day when the plane left New Zealand, but chances are that it will be at least 15 degrees below zero on the ice runway called Williams Field.

There is plenty of food aboard, but no hostesses to serve it in colorful plastic trays. Self-service is the rule; and — except for coffee — it is strictly a cold meal. There are crackers and bread, several kinds of meat and cheese, and hard-boiled eggs. There may be a 10-pound can of strawberry jam, too, with some fresh apples or preserved peaches for dessert. Eating picnic style, everybody agrees that it couldn't be better.

At some point, one of the men remarks about the sun; and soon everybody is discussing it. It may be 3 A.M. or 11 P.M., but the sun is there — turning the white sheet below into a dazzling pool of light that is hard to look at, even through sunglasses. Barring storms, the sun will be with them now 24 hours a day — until winter comes or until they return to the "real world" they have left behind them.

The first glimpse of land is exciting, and somewhat of a relief. As a black sliver on the horizon grows slowly into the rocky ridge of Cape Adare, every new visitor feels a strange thrill. There *is* a continent there after all; the geography books are correct. It seems like an original, personal discovery.

Flights on the Antarctic Airline are gradually becoming easier and more comfortable. Shuttle planes from Christchurch can land at McMurdo, pause for two hours or less, and head right back to New Zealand. The smaller but faster C-130 Hercules carries many of the passengers now, and the bulky Globemaster is generally re-

The U. S. Navy's C-130 has both wheels and skis, so that it can be used on land, ice or snow runways.

served for the heavier jobs. In any case the contrast between modern-day planes and the early days of Antarctic aviation is amazing.

Roald Amundsen once told Byrd that Antarctica would be truly conquered only by air. In 1902, Scott had used a captive balloon to survey the Ross Ice Shelf, and the German explorer Erich von Drygalski had done the same near the present Russian station of Mirnyy. Amundsen himself had crossed the North Pole in a dirigible and undoubtedly considered using lighter-than-air craft in the south polar regions as well. But airplanes were even faster and more versatile. Only a series of mechanical problems kept them from being introduced to the Antarctic earlier than the fall of 1928.

That year, Sir Hubert Wilkins and an Alaskan mail pilot named C. B. Eielson made the first flights from Deception Island in a wheeled monoplane. They took off from a cindery airstrip not much wider than a two-lane highway, but they made aerial explorations along 600 miles of coastline.

Unfortunately, the view from the air can sometimes be deceptive. Momentarily losing their bearings, they mistook a large island for the mainland and decided that the Antarctic Peninsula was actually cut off from the rest of the continent. About 10 years passed before a combination of land and air explorations corrected the error.

Meanwhile, across the continent, Richard E. Byrd was preparing an expedition which would win the admiration of the world. He had brought with him *three* airplanes, all equipped with skis so they could take off from snow. One, a Fokker, was caught on the ground in a storm and dashed to pieces. The second, a single-engined Fairchild, was used only for preliminary studies of the mountains south of his base near the Bay of Whales. The third, an all-metal Ford with three motors, was intended to take him over the South Pole and back.

Byrd set up a fuel and supply base near the foot of the Liv Glacier. His preparations for the polar trip were painstaking. At the end of each test flight, every drop of oil and gasoline was drained from the engine to keep it from hardening in the cold. The plane itself was jammed with emergency equipment: tents, sleeping bags, portable stoves and fuel. There was barely room for the four-man crew.

Byrd, the navigator, had already flown over the North Pole. An ordinary magnetic compass was useless in the polar regions, and the gyroscopic kind could not be trusted completely; so he used a "sun compass." This instrument had been devised by Albert H. Bumstead of the National Geographic Society. It worked like a sundial in reverse, with the shadow indicating a north-south line when adjusted by an accurate timepiece.

On the historic flight, tension was high as the heavily

loaded plane neared the top of the unexplored glacier. At 9,600 feet Byrd's plane strained and spat, but could go no higher. Dumping fuel was out of the question; that would put the Pole beyond their range. Without hesitation the determined explorers heaved their two huge bags of emergency rations through the trapdoor in the bottom of the plane and watched them split open far below. The sacrifice was successful, and the plane rose proudly above the lip of the glacier.

With the smooth polar plateau beneath them, the rest of the flight south was almost an anticlimax. Returning by a slightly different route so that they could photograph more new territory, they descended along the Axel Heiberg Glacier and paused at the bottom just long enough to refuel. Then back to their main base — Little America — racing ahead of a furious storm.

Antarctic aviation stimulated the explorations of many nations during the 1930's, but the most important single exploit was probably the transcontinental flight of Lincoln Ellsworth in 1935. This American adventurer brought with him a specially designed, low-winged Northrop equipped with skis. His idea was that if the weather became threatening he would simply land and dig in until the storm blew over. Even though Ellsworth's route from the Antarctic Peninsula to Byrd's base on the Ross Ice Shelf was a "shortcut" from the Atlantic to the Pacific coasts, it showed that his plan was sound. He crossed the frozen desert in four hops.

After World War II, the United States Navy organized a 4,000-man campaign to open the Antarctic. The name assigned to the program was Operation Highjump. It used 13 ships, including two seaplane tenders and the aircraft carrier *Philippine Sea*. Six two-engine R4D transports (the Navy equivalent of the familiar DC-3 airliner) flew mission after mission. Half a dozen big Martin PBM flying boats and the same number of helicopters were also used. During this all-out effort, Byrd made his second flight over the Pole.

The R4Ds had wheels which fit through slots in the skis during carrier takeoffs, but which could be removed when operating from the snow. Tractors helped smooth the flying strips on shore. If the planes had to operate from unprepared snow they could get an extra boost from JATO bottles (the letters stand for Jet Assisted Takeoff).

Byrd's helicopters — powerful offsprings of the autogyro which he had used for a while during his 1933–35 expedition — were used chiefly as scouts. They warned of ice conditions and located stretches of open water which the PBMs could use on their photo-mapping flights. Almost two-thirds of the entire Antarctic coast was charted, and Navy fliers discovered a snow-free oasis of at least 100 square miles.

Once again, however, the difficulties of using aerial observations alone as the basis of maps became obvious. During the following season (1947–48), a modest force of two Navy icebreakers returned to Antarctica. Using helicopters to a greater extent than ever before, they pinpointed the location of certain landmarks in order to help interpret past and future photography. During the same season, a private expedition headed by Captain Finn Ronne also used ski planes.

After this, however, the United States withdrew from Antarctica for almost a decade. But seaplanes and amphibians were used by the nations interested in the Antarctic Peninsula, and Argentina — which earlier had made the first flight over Antarctic territory from another continent — used a long-range Air Force plane from the South American mainland to drop mail and supplies to an icebound station in Antarctica.

117

The stage was set for a massive aerial assault on the unknown continent itself during the IGY. Aircraft had operated along every coast . . . on wheels, skis and floats. They had climbed the inner plateau, and they had operated without real landing fields. They had reached the Antarctic nonstop from another continent, and they had been used to resupply men on the ground. Nevertheless, the actual use of planes in connection with the International Geophysical Year of 1957–58 combined and extended these accomplishments in a way that changed the face of Antarctica. Millions of square miles of inland territory were explored.

Preparations began almost two years in advance with a flight of four Navy transports from New Zealand. Even the wheeled planes had no difficulty landing on the relatively smooth bay ice, which had already been inspected by ship. Soon flights were crisscrossing the continent almost routinely. Since the shore base at McMurdo was still under construction, the planes refueled directly from the tanker USS *Nespelen.*

According to the plan of this first Operation Deep Freeze, almost 100 men spent the winter at McMurdo Sound. In mid-October, 1956, by the time it seemed safe to fly again, they had cleared the snow from a 6,000-foot strip of bay ice. At that time of year the ice is from 25 to 40 feet thick. Thus, months in advance of the first icebreaker's arrival, McMurdo Sound was open again to traffic from the rest of the world. It was still too early to call the operation an airline, but at least the Antarctic Airlift had begun.

Two weeks later, Rear Admiral George J. Dufek and a party of six others in a thirteen-year-old R4D became the first men since Scott to stand at the geographic South Pole. Flying over the Pole was one thing, but landing there was another; it would be almost like landing on the moon. The men knew what the surface looked like, but they couldn't be sure how it would react to the landing. Would frozen ridges of snow trip and shatter the skis? Or was there a chance they would sink so deep that they couldn't take off again? What would happen if the motors quit in the −57-degree temperature?

The landing proved safe enough. For three-quarters of an hour the Deep Freeze commander and his men planted radar reflectors, set up a flag, and inspected the snow surface — until waxy, yellowish-white spots on their faces told them that frostbite was setting in. They scrambled aboard the plane (whose engines had never stopped running, for fear they might freeze), and with a mighty kick in the tail from 15 JATO bottles the plane shuddered back into the air.

That season, the Seabees of Deep Freeze II got some tips from Army experts on how to improve their bay-ice runway at McMurdo Sound. The holes which develop after heavy use are filled with a mixture of ice chips, snow and water. In freezing weather, this ice cement works fine; but nothing can prevent the disaster of a summer thaw. New Year's Day might find the hard work of the winter crew floating out to sea.

An alternate runway has now been built on the snow nearby. The Navy engineers who designed it used the same technique that produced a 150-acre parking lot for the Winter Olympics at Squaw Valley, California. Three successive layers of snow were added to the ground layer, smoothed out, packed down and frozen. By the time the construction team had finished, the snow runway stood two feet above the surface around it. The height discourages new snow from drifting across the airfield, and the separate layers give added strength.

In some areas of the Antarctic, of course, it is possible to land on bare ground. The dry valleys are generally too

119

The surface of the sea ice at McMurdo is scraped smooth, and then a 5,000-pound roller is used to compact the loose snow on top.

rocky for anything but a light plane; but a 1,700-foot dirt field was cleared of boulders and has been in operation for some time at Marble Point, on the western side of McMurdo Sound. The Australian and Russian stations on the other side of Antarctica are also located in the general vicinity of flat, solid land; but no effort has been made to convert these areas into suitable landing strips.

Williams Field, the principal southern terminal for the Antarctic Airline, is normally open for business from September through February, although it has handled emergency flights at other times. Planes have even landed there in the middle of the Antarctic winter, when the edges of the runway had to be marked by drums of blazing fuel oil; but this is unusual. It takes about a month each year to scrape the bay ice smooth, fill in the potholes, and lay out the runway.

Williams Field is equipped with radio and radar systems which permit planes to land safely regardless of fog or low-hanging clouds. A cluster of temporary buildings there includes supply shacks, a kitchen, and a dining hall, as well as sleeping quarters for crews who don't want to travel four miles across the ice of McMurdo Sound to the base on shore. At the peak of the resupply season, pilots are on call almost constantly — using every valuable minute of good flying weather for their trips to the inland stations.

The airmen refer to their cargoes casually as "beans, bodies and bolts." These were the ingredients of the first station in history to be set up on a year-round basis at the very bottom of the earth.

The job could not have been done without airplanes. More than a million and a half pounds of equipment were parachuted to the band at the South Pole during their first season in 1956–57 — stoves, building materials, food, scientific instruments and even tractors. Today, the

121

The C-130 can deliver big vehicles to inland stations.

ski-equipped C-130s deliver more than that to Pole Station each year. Flights average almost one a day. More than 200 flights a season are now made from McMurdo to Byrd Station, delivering over 2,500 tons of men and supplies.

During the 1962–63 season, an entire new outpost was set up by airlift in less than three weeks. Named Eights Station (in honor of James Eights, the first American scientist to visit the Antarctic), this prefabricated base at the inner edge of the Antarctic Peninsula is the most difficult of all to resupply from McMurdo. Each flight is roughly equivalent to the entire length of Lincoln Ellsworth's epic trip, except that today's planes sometimes return along the same path without landing at all. The weather is so bad that the parachute drops must frequently be directed by radar rather than visual sighting.

Antarctic flying is still tricky. Ice tends to coat the wings, gusty winds pummel the planes, and magnetic storms often interrupt radio communications. Although some cabins are not pressurized, every plane to the Pole must fly at an altitude of more than 10,000 feet just to clear the towering central plateau.

A helicopter lifts supplies to a hard-to-reach plateau.

Navigation offers the same difficulties faced by Byrd. Modern fliers use the familiar Navy system of shooting the sun with a sextant, but they also overlay the map with a network of squares which provide artificial directions. From the South Pole, any way you head is north; and the conventional meridians would be too confusing to work with.

The most peculiar hazard of all in Antarctic flying is called a whiteout. It takes place when there is a slight overcast and the clouds are fairly low. Sunlight filtering through the clouds is reflected back and forth between the clouds and the snow. Finally, with light coming equally from all directions, all shadows disappear and the surface seems to melt into the sky.

A whiteout is not the same as fog. If there were enough familiar objects in sight you might still keep your bearings. But the blank surface of snow and ice gives no clues. Just looking out of the window, it's impossible to tell whether you're flying in a circle, upside down or straight up. Pilots say it is "like flying through a bowl of milk." That is, except when a whiteout takes place during a wind storm. Then it's more like flying inside a ping-pong ball.

Keeping the planes in shape takes ingenuity as well as skill. With the nearest supply depot thousands of miles away, parts from a DC-3 have been used to repair a C-130.

Fuel saving calls for more brainwork. Neptune patrol planes flew their photoreconnaissance missions regularly at 19,000 feet until someone discovered that they could cover more square miles per gallon by climbing to 25,000 feet. They used more fuel that way, but their photos covered far more territory. However, there was a hitch: To get to the higher altitude, the Neptunes had to use twin jets besides their two normal engines. They did so until one pilot got into trouble and lost the use of one jet engine. When he found that he could limp along quite

A heater hose is used
to defrost a plane for a midwinter Antarctic flight.

satisfactorily, he passed the word to his buddies. After that, the photo planes always used both jets and both engines to reach their service altitude of 25,000 feet, then routinely cut off one jet for the rest of the mission.

Operating from an ice runway offers some difficulties. The wind keeps snow removal crews at work constantly.

A sudden rise in temperature will leave cargo crates standing in puddles of water, and a quick freeze may cement them to the field. During "warm" years, the men at Williams Field face the prospect of being chased off completely to the alternate field, dragging buildings and equipment with them.

Despite all the problems, there have been relatively few fatal accidents; and Antarctic explorers have gradually built up a large and varied aerial fleet. A single C-124 now carries about five times the load that almost spilled Admiral Byrd's pioneer Ford into the Liv Glacier. The latest C-130s have managed to take off from South Africa, fly all the way across the ocean, and then continue across the entire continent before landing at McMurdo Sound.

Light aircraft like the Otter, which built its reputation as a "bush plane" in the Canadian Arctic, will probably always have their place. The same goes for seaplanes.

**Light plane takes off
after delivering biologists to a scientific campsite.**

Turbine-powered helicopters help, too. Capable of reaching almost inaccessible mountain crags up to 13,000 feet, these big, six-seat whirlybirds lift surveyors from peak to peak and have even reached the Pole itself.

Aerial charting remains a problem. The "tallest mountain in Antarctica" — 20,000-foot "Mt. Vinson" — was erased from the maps when ground study and further flights showed that the fliers' eyes and cameras had fooled them. (The "discovery" was really 13,850-foot Mt. Sidley, 70 miles to the northwest.)

There are other American planes, too, as well as a similar variety of aircraft from other nations. Many of the latter have landed at McMurdo, which forms a convenient gateway to the continent. Furthermore, the reports from weather satellites have begun to benefit the New Zealand-McMurdo route considerably since a special receiving station was set up at Christchurch.

True to Amundsen's prophecy, aviation has shrunk Antarctica. If the land is not yet tame, at least it is more manageable. Few men who visit the Antarctic these days come away without at least one color photograph of deep blue sky, brilliant white ice, and the orange tail markings of a silver transport plane. The sight is common, but the contrast still seems exciting.

CHAPTER EIGHT

A Visit to the Big City

The road across the bay ice from Williams Field to the main base of McMurdo is marked by small flags; and its route may change from week to week. When oil and grease turn the ice road black, its surface soaks up heat from the sun more quickly. Rather than take a chance on melting through, the U. S. Navy then reroutes the highway across some fresh white stretch of ice.

As the bright yellow "weasel" which serves as an airport taxi nears the base, it passes a series of five red and white signs. The verse style is familiar:

> Use our cream
> And we betcha . . .
> Girls won't wait,
> They'll come and getcha.
> BURMA SHAVE!

It's a fit greeting to McMurdo Sound — the all-male metropolis of the Deep, Deep, Deepfreeze South. McMurdo is a busy place, a transportation center. And it is

McMurdo Station is at the southern tip of
Ross Island, at the edge of the Ice Shelf.

typically American, for all its bearded inhabitants and
their strange surroundings. In spite of the hardships im-
posed by nature, it is a place where men rarely lose their
sense of humor.

None of the 75 buildings at McMurdo is more than
one story high. There are orange, boxlike shelters which
look like king-sized packing crates. Their walls are plywood, insulated with fiberglass and lined with aluminum.
There are olive-drab Jamesway huts too, each shaped like
a big barrel sliced lengthwise. These are less substantial
and less wind-resistant — nothing but a couple of layers of
canvas and insulation stretched over a wooden frame.
And there are some special structures, too — like the
bulb-shaped weather shack and the big hangar which
serves as a repair shop.

129

McMurdo Station is Antarctica's "Boom Town." The long low building in the foreground is the dining hall.

A walk up the slushy, rutted main street gives a profile of life at the base. On one side, for example, is the long, low mess hall. Open the door and you find what looks like a closet . . . and another door. This is typical of U. S. buildings in the Antarctic; you must always pass through a double set of doors to go in or out. If doors opened directly to the outside, it would be harder to keep the heat in and the snow out.

Inside the mess hall there is bound to be a line of McMurdans and visitors. The dining hall was built originally to take care of about 250 people, but the summer population these days is more than four times that number, and you cannot escape the crowds. Four meals are served each day: breakfast from 5:30 to 7:15, lunch from 11:15 to 1 P.M., supper from 5:15 to 7, and "late supper" from 11:30 to midnight. In between, of course, there is always coffee.

Except for breakfast — which includes the usual morning fare of bacon and eggs, cereal, hotcakes, etc. — every meal at McMurdo looks like a multi-course banquet. Here's a typical luncheon menu:

SPLIT PEA OR FRENCH ONION SOUP
(WITH SALTINES & CROUTONS)
BOILED SMOKED HAM WITH PINEAPPLE
FRIED LIVER & ONIONS
* * *

CANDIED SWEET POTATOES   WHIPPED POTATOES
BUTTERED COLLARD GREENS
CREAMED CARROTS   BUTTERED BROCCOLI
CORN NIBLETS
* * *

APPLE PIE AND BLUEBERRY PIE
ICE CREAM
COOKIES   FRUIT JELLO   WHIPPED CREAM
* * *

POWDERED MILK   COFFEE   TEA   HOT CHOCOLATE
* * *

VITAMIN PILLS

The choice of ham and liver is not an "either-or" proposition. Many of the men will take both . . . along with soup, three or four different vegetables, both kinds of pie (à la mode), and some Jello with whipped cream. Oh yes, and a few vitamin pills to top it off. In the cold of Antarctica, the body burns extra food to keep warm. Long hours of outdoor work in bulky clothing adds to the appetite. The Navy, which operates all U. S. bases in Antarctica, encourages each man there to take in at least

5,000 calories a day — more than twice the average of a healthy adult in the United States.

On overland traverses, rations are stepped up even more. During the two months it took to set up Army-Navy Drive each member of the working party was allotted an average of seven and a half pounds of food a day. Nevertheless, almost every one of the men lost weight.

About the only thing which doesn't seem to be plentiful at the McMurdo dining room is water. This might seem strange on a continent covered by most of the world's ice, but remember that ice can be turned into water only by applying heat. Heat means fuel, and fuel is scarce. For almost 10 years McMurdo's entire water supply came from melting snow. Thirty times a day, a 15-ton, caterpillar-treaded Traxcavator would shuttle back and forth between the camp's five snow melters and a bank of fresh, clean snow more than half a mile away. The snow, melted in a big oil-fired boiler, produced water which was gray, oily . . . and scarce. Drinking water could never be wasted; and even water for washing was in such short supply that showers were rationed. The installation in 1965 of a plant to distill salt water makes things easier; at least it puts the men on an even footing with the penguins — who have been getting along on seawater for years.

Up the street from the mess hall is a row of barracks. Most of them are decorated with good-natured signs like HAROLD'S CLUB, THE LITTLE BARREL BAR, PENGUIN PALACE and THE ROYAL HAWAIIAN. Alongside one is a wad of packing material which has been dyed green. The sign above it says PLEASE KEEP OFF THE GRASS.

Inside, the barracks are crowded and somewhat dreary. Cans of melted snow provide a little humidity, but the atmosphere is still as dry as dust. Wet boot prints on the rough wooden floor dry up in a few minutes. The buildings don't show the spit and polish of most naval stations.

McMurdo is especially crowded during the summer.

First of all, only some of the residents of McMurdo are military; the rest are civilians. Secondly, this is a field base rather than a showplace. Nevertheless, the men take turns at being "house mouse." This means doing the inside chores and keeping things generally tidy. Neatness helps morale.

The beds are regulation Army double-decker style — which offers an interesting choice of temperature when you try to go to sleep. Because of poor circulation in the huts, the upper bunk is always too hot and the lower bunk

133

is invariably too cold. Antarctic veterans generally pick a lower bunk if they get the choice. They know that you can always pile your clothes on top of the heavy woolen blankets in order to stay warm. That's better than sweltering in the stuffy upper deck.

Clothing, incidentally, is an important part of the way of life at McMurdo. You can usually feel comfortable in a sport shirt and slacks as long as you stay inside; but getting ready for a venture into the great outdoors takes time. The idea is to cover yourself with as many layers of clothing as possible, since the air space between layers gives extra insulation. Strangely enough, sunglasses are important, too. Without them, the steady glare of snow and ice could damage your vision permanently.

Every visitor is issued pounds and pounds of special clothing before embarking on the Antarctic Airline. It starts with long, waffle-weave underwear and heavy socks; and it isn't unusual at an Antarctic base for a man to wear two pairs of each at one time. Two pairs of trousers (one nylon, one wool) and two long-sleeved shirts are also suggested — topped by a field jacket and a parka. On very cold days gloves are worn in double layers, too — one set wool and the outer shells of leather. To keep your feet comfortable even at 60 below, there are specially designed thermal boots. The clumsy white "Mickey Mouse shoes" may not be beautiful, but they certainly are warm.

Sailors and scientists who visit the Antarctic often develop some pet ideas about clothing. One may insist that the only hood worth having is one lined with wolverine fur; for some reason this kind doesn't trap moisture from your breath and end up full of ice crystals. Another will say that a knitted face mask is best, while still another prefers to get along with just a sporty red-and-white cap. Some Americans envy the shiny quilted jackets issued by the British and New Zealanders, in bright colors like cherry-red and grass-green. But the reason for the colorful garb actually has nothing to do with fashion tastes. The colors are just supposed to be easier to spot at a distance in snow and ice.

Back outside on the main street of McMurdo, the next stop is the chapel. This is where Cardinal Spellman offered Christmas Mass in 1963. It is a neat white wooden building with a small, square bell steeple. Most of the men call it the Chapel of the Snows. The chapel also serves as a base library, and the chaplain doubles as librarian. The collection of some 3,000 volumes ranges from Antarctic history to detective stories.

Chapel of the Snows

Beyond the chapel is the Admiral's residence. It is a little larger than some of the other buildings, and it is handsomely furnished. But its chief distinction is the big front window. It is the only picture window at McMurdo.

McMurdo Sound is a complete community, even to having dial telephones. There is a barber shop (or at least a barber chair), a dentist, a bank, a small hospital and a post office. The Zip Code is 96648.

The general store at McMurdo sells everything from candy to cameras — as long as it's in stock. It even sells postcards and souvenirs. One of the favorite items is a set of cuff links which look like tiny penguins sealed in ice cubes. They are made in Providence, Rhode Island.

The luxuries seem so natural at McMurdo that they are taken for granted. It takes a shortage of some item — a little thing like talcum powder or dental floss, perhaps — to remind you that the next cargo ship may not arrive for a month or two.

Because almost everything on the continent of Antarctica has been imported, any sort of material can seem precious. Wooden boxes are never discarded casually; with some ingenuity they may turn into tables or shelves. Once a supply officer even solved a critical shortage of teletype tape by using ordinary brown wrapping paper. Miles of the tape were made by using a lathe and a razor blade to slice down wide paper rolls.

Even if everyone finally gives up on some item and throws it away, chances are that it may be recovered from the scrap heap. You see, McMurdo's garbage dump is located on sea ice which drops it into the sound only once a year or so. It isn't too unusual to see somebody picking through the rubbish in search of an old piece of equipment or bit of metal which was tossed away several months before but now suddenly seems valuable again.

The closest link with home is the "ham shack." The

Ham radio is a link with home.

men of McMurdo operate a powerful amateur radio station with the call letters KC4USV. The walls of the building are papered with hundreds of "QSL cards," indicating contacts with stations all over the globe. When conditions are right, a man at McMurdo may even speak directly with his family by means of a "phone patch." Here's how it works:

Suppose a man from Newark, N. J., wants to talk to his folks. The radio operator at McMurdo broadcasts an appeal to anyone in that area who happens to be listening, and pauses for a response. He may be lucky enough to pick up a "ham" from the city itself. Or maybe his contact will be in Trenton, New York City or some other place near Newark. The radio operator in the United States puts in a phone call to the Antarctican's family, and the radio-telephone conversation can proceed. Obviously each man at McMurdo has to await his turn, except in case of an emergency.

There are other recreations at McMurdo, too. Many of the buildings have hi-fi and stereo sets, so that recorded music is played throughout the working day. Lots of classics . . . very little rock 'n' roll. And there are movies every night.

McMurdo is a typical military base in some ways. There is an officers' club, another for chief petty officers, and a third for enlisted men. Each one is decorated with travel posters, artificial palm trees and other reminders of pleasant surroundings. There is also a special barracks for VIPs — Very Important Persons. It has single-decker bunks instead of double-decker bunks, but the only other difference between it and the others is the sign on the door. Being the fanciest "hotel" on the ice shelf, it is naturally called the Ross Hilton.

McMurdo is a noisy town, especially during the summer season. Not one minute of the 24-hour daylight can be wasted, and the tired groans of bulldozers and the clatter of tracked cargo carriers can be heard in its streets around the clock. The huts are by no means soundproof.

Between the noise outside and the midnight sun streaming through their unshaded windows, many of McMurdo's

An "entrance hall" the size of a telephone booth helps to keep heat from leaking out of a hut when the door is opened.

residents have trouble getting to sleep. The problem is so common that they have given it a special name: "the big eye." Bulging, bloodshot eyes, ringed with dark circles, are an unfortunate trademark of the Antarctic summer visitors.

Perhaps the men of McMurdo are lucky that there is so much work to do during the summer season. Construction of some sort is usually going on. Bulldozers and tractors are kept running steadily, all day long and seven days a week. The 12- to 14-hour shifts help any man to relax readily when his workday is over — even if the sun *is* still shining.

Relaxing at McMurdo after a hard day's work

There is a newspaper at McMurdo, but its publication schedule is not always regular. Hence its name — the *McMurdo Sometimer*. It reports such exciting events as interstation chess tournaments and the annual Memorial Day Hot Rod Race. Top speed for the vehicles in this race — weasels, Sno-Cats, power wagons, etc. — is rarely over 15 miles an hour; but competition is still fun.

Americans anywhere love sports, and they refuse to be daunted by the Antarctic weather. They have organized

Lack of oxygen, the weight of heavy clothing, and 33-below-zero temperature doesn't spoil a football game's excitement.

football and baseball games in the snow — mostly for laughs; and one group of sailors even braved several blizzards to build a skating rink on the ice shelf. There is also an indoor gym at McMurdo equipped with weights, barbells, wrestling mats and boxing gloves. A bowling alley was installed by the Seabees several years ago, but during the summer season it is covered over and converted into an extra barracks for the enlarged population.

When the last plane of the season leaves, the atmosphere at McMurdo changes. The 24-hour days merge into a steady twilight, and more of the men's leisure time is spent indoors. The "University of Antarctica" begins its informal courses in history, language and science. And gradually the men begin to feel their isolation. Carefully screened on the basis of personality tests, the wintering-over crew will be able to withstand the tension. But the four-month night is something they will never forget. The raising of the flag at the next sunrise in late August is something everyone looks forward to.

Elsewhere on the continent, the story is much the same: Hallett Station, 350 miles north of McMurdo, is similar in appearance but smaller. It began in 1957 as a year-round station; but since February, 1965, it has become strictly a summer station. Located in an area which was once a penguin rookery, Hallett is surrounded by a low wire fence to keep the "natives" out from under foot. The United States shares the operation of Hallett with New Zealand, and the staff represents both countries.

On the other side of Antarctica, Eights Station is far more compact. It consists of 11 prefabricated units, each slightly smaller than a boxcar. Eight of these are arranged in twin rows of four each, connected by a covered hallway which is covered at both ends. The result is one big building. The other three units are separated by a little distance for the purpose of carrying out special scientific projects. Eights Station is supposed to be a mobile station, which means it can be taken down and set up again.

Beyond Eights is the smallest and most northerly of all the U. S. stations — an outpost of only two buildings on Anvers Island, just off the Antarctic Peninsula. Called

THE BUILDING OF BYRD STATION

1. A Peter Snow Miller digs a deep pit in the snow.

2. The walls are scraped smooth.

Palmer Station, it was opened early in 1965 to carry on research in the plant life and geology of this relatively warm region (where the year-round temperature averages a toasty 20 degrees).

The other extreme in climate is South Pole Station, where winter temperatures dip as much as 110 degrees below zero. It is the most remote base. Built during the IGY, it has been enlarged gradually to include about a dozen buildings. Most of them are interconnected by tunnels, and the major part of the station is itself under the snow.

The most modern American "city" in Antarctica is Byrd Station. It was built by digging a main tunnel and seven branches, bridging them with covered arches, and then topping the whole complex with crushed ice and snow. When the topping froze, the subsurface city had a roof as solid as concrete.

3. Steel arches are set in place, and prefabricated buildings are assembled inside the sub-zero tunnels.

Inside Byrd Station the buildings in which the men live and work are on platforms which keep them two to three feet off the tunnel floor. At least four feet of clear space is allowed at the top and on all sides, so that heat from the buildings will not melt the surrounding snow. The prefabricated buildings are actually built like refrigerators — except that they're intended to keep the heat in instead of out. An elaborate system of fans draws in fresh air constantly through vents in the snow ceiling. In all, Byrd Station consists of more than a mile of tunnels. They are 20 to 36 feet wide and about three stories deep. Bathed in shimmering blue-white light, snug from the storms above, the sleek comfort of Byrd Station is probably a preview of things to come in Antarctica. Skyscrapers may be the mark of progress on the other six continents; but in Antarctica the trend is toward subways.

CHAPTER NINE

The Atomic Age Meets the Ice Age

Nuclear energy means different things to different
people. To military leaders it means bombs.
Doctors think of it as a tool to diagnose and cure illness.
In Antarctica it means more showers, safer heat, flush
toilets and extra weather reports.

On December 14, 1961 — 50 years to the day after
Roald Amundsen raised his flag over the South Pole —

146

McMurdo's nuclear reactor power plant is housed in these buildings, with condensers on platform outside.

the USS *Arneb* began to unload a cargo which opened a new chapter in Antarctic development. Part of it was a collection of tanks and boxes, which were assembled into the continent's first nuclear reactor. The *Arneb* also carried a smaller atomic package — a midget generator. Its purpose was to operate an automatic weather station buried along the edge of the Ross Ice Shelf.

The two nuclear power devices are quite different, both in size and operation. The reactor plant produces a million and a half watts of continuous electricity — enough to light all the lights and run all the electrical equipment at McMurdo Sound, yet with enough heat left over to purify millions of gallons of seawater annually. The weather station generator puts out only 10 watts, but it works without any moving parts and needs nobody to look after it. Both systems are designed to operate for many years.

The reactor power plant now sits on a small plateau near the base of Observation Hill, overlooking the main area of McMurdo Station. The site was prepared during the 1960–61 season, when two great pits were blasted out

A section of the nuclear reactor power plant is unloaded onto the bay ice at McMurdo Sound.

One man can operate the console of the reactor.

of the rock on the far side of the plateau. One is occupied by the tanks which make up the nuclear part of the power plant, buried now under tons of crushed gravel to block off nuclear radiation. The others will someday enclose a second reactor . . . for McMurdo expects to grow.

Sections of the big power plant were hauled on sleds up a twisting, slushy road to the plateau on Observation Hill. There, under the supervision of the engineers who had designed and tested it in the United States, Navy Seabees put the "do-it-yourself" plant back together again. It took them only 11 weeks to get it in operating order.

The heart of the system is a fuel core the size of an oil

drum. It is made up of about 750 hollow steel tubes, all bundled together. Inside the wall of each tube is a material containing fissionable uranium, which produces heat when the reactor is turned on. Water is pumped through and around the tubes constantly, absorbing the heat as fast as it is produced. This water is kept under pressure in a strong metal loop; it never turns to steam, but it does pass through a series of U-shaped tubes inside a boiler. There, water under lower pressure in adjoining pipes picks up the heat and is changed into steam. The steam turns the blades of a turbine to generate electricity, then is piped outside to a condenser, where cold air changes it back into water, starting the cycle all over again.

Most of the plant's operations are automatic, but at least two trained crewmen must be on hand whenever the reactor is running. To start it, the operator checks the dials on the L-shaped control board and shifts a switch marked ROD MOTION CONTROL to the OUT position. Fifteen feet below ground level, near the bottom of the water-filled reactor tank, powerful magnets slowly lift the control rods out of the core. As they are removed, the rate of fission speeds up and heat is produced.

If anything should go wrong at any time, the electromagnets cut off automatically. The control rods fall back into place and the nuclear reaction stops.

The power plant is a great attraction for sightseers at McMurdo, but naturally it wasn't put there just as a novelty. One big advantage it has is that nuclear fuel is easy to carry. A single fuel core — only three feet high and less than two feet in diameter — would last for at least two years even if it were operated at full power 24 hours a day. To produce the same amount of electricity with diesel generators would take more than two million gallons of oil. That would take up precious cargo space on an Ant-

The old and the new: Tens of thousands of oil drums are replaced
by a single fuel core in the McMurdo nuclear power plant.

arctic convoy — room which might better be used for aviation gasoline or other essential supplies.

So far, McMurdo Sound is the only base in Antarctica which has a nuclear power plant; but there has been a great deal of talk about installing other plants at inland stations. It will make sense to do so, especially as the inland stations grow and as nuclear reactor plants become simpler to operate.

Getting diesel fuel from McMurdo Sound to inland stations by air has always been slow and costly. If the fuel drums were to be dropped from a plane like the C-124 (which cannot land on snow) they could not just be thrown out of a window. Preparing an airdrop takes time. Cargo parachutes will support four fuel drums at once, but something still must be done to keep the impact from damaging the steel barrels. Each set of four drums is strapped to a platform, made of alternating layers of plywood and folded cardboard. The platform — which cannot be reused — cushions the shock of landing.

A fueldrop is a demanding operation. As the big plane approaches its destination the atmosphere inside it changes from quiet routine to the tenseness of a bombing mission. The pilot, navigator and dropmaster exchange clipped messages by intercom; and the temperature drops sharply when the clamshell doors in the plane's belly swing open. Sub-zero wind whips the hands of the crewmen as they undo the last of the straps holding each set of drums in place. Then comes the moment when the fuel loads go clattering down the metal roller ramp and disappear into the white gaping hole. As the plane circles, the brightly colored parachutes drift earthward in a narrow line. Far below, men scramble about to collect the precious black drums.

On missions like this, seven crewmen used to take a $2,000,000 plane more than 800 miles to deliver a few thousand gallons of diesel oil at a time to the South Pole. Their nine-hour round-trip flight would have to be repeated about 500 times to provide Pole Station with as much energy as is locked inside the single nuclear core at McMurdo.

The delivery job can be done a little more easily now with ski planes. They are faster, and they can deliver fuel in bulk instead of in heavy individual drums. But fuel needs are too great to be satisfied forever by an airlift of any kind; diesel oil still makes up more than two-thirds of all the cargo needed to keep a station going. Nuclear power plants, built like the one at McMurdo in sections which can be reassembled quickly on the spot, seem to be the best long-range answer. Once in place, they need little resupply.

Power lines are strung at McMurdo Sound to make it the first atomic city in the world.

This is how McMurdo got its water supply before the nuclear plant permitted the installation of a salt water converter.

Even at McMurdo, it was impractical to think of installing a plumbing system as long as all water had to come from oil-burning snow melters. But nuclear energy has provided a generous new water supply by supplying heat to the new saltwater evaporator. A heated sewage system at McMurdo is another Atomic Age "first."

While fuel and electricity were so strictly rationed, certain equipment simply could not be used; there was a perpetual power shortage. Nuclear energy changes that, too. McMurdo's atomic plant has given it several times as much electrical energy as it ever got from all its diesels put together.

154

There is still another big advantage — perhaps the most important of all. The use of nuclear energy reduces the terrible danger of fire in the Antarctic.

Fire is probably a greater threat there than anywhere else on earth. Most buildings are made of wood and canvas, and high winds can spread flames quickly. Furthermore, if a fire should start during a wintry blizzard, the men whose shelter is threatened have no real means of escape. To be left outside in a storm may be fatal, yet they cannot stay inside either unless they manage to extinguish the fire quickly. Even if water is readily available (and it usually isn't) it may be almost useless. Water freezes too easily and you can't quench a fire with icicles. Instead, the best solution is usually to try to snuff out the fire with sand or powdered chemicals.

There have been several fires at McMurdo Sound, as well as at Hallett Station, Amundsen-Scott (South Pole)

Dry chemicals are poured into portable fire extinguishers to help fight a 1961 blaze in McMurdo's parachute building. Nuclear energy reduces the danger of fire by eliminating oil stoves.

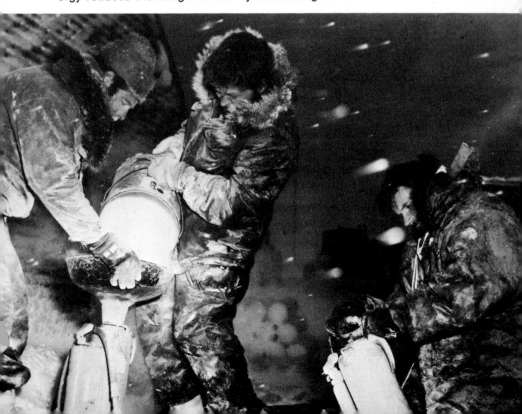

Station, and at the Australians' auroral base near Mawson. In 1960, eight Russian scientists lost their lives when a blaze wiped out their hut at the Russians' Mirnyy Station. Many of these disasters have been traced to oil stoves; and the men at McMurdo are happy that such stoves have now been replaced by electrical heaters. But the switch could not have taken place if it were not for the nuclear power plant. Before it arrived, electricity was too scarce.

The smaller nuclear generator in the Antarctic weather station provides safety in quite a different way. Air operations in the Antarctic will always involve unusual risk until some way is developed to produce continuous weather reports all along the path of flight. It is unlikely that there will ever be enough manned stations to do this, so unmanned automatic weather monitors seem to hold the key.

Battery-operated weather stations have been in use for many years, but they sometimes freeze up. They also pose another problem. Batteries must be replaced every few months; and in Antarctica this isn't easy. For this reason, a small nuclear generator which turns out power continuously for 10 years or more is a big help.

The first such generator is called SNAP 7-C. The "7-C" is just a model number; the other letters stand for "Systems for Nuclear Auxiliary Power." SNAP 7-C operates in the same way as the atomic generators which have been launched into space on satellites, placed in lighthouses and navigation buoys, and even dropped to the bottom of the ocean to operate electronic equipment there. Here's how:

The whole generator is a stubby cylinder about 21 inches high. Inside it are four capsules of a radioactive compound, each of which takes up less room than a couple of flashlight batteries. The radioactive material decays spontaneously, causing enough heat to keep the metal block surrounding it at approximately 900 degrees Fahrenheit. Thermocouples convert the difference in temperature between the insulated inner shell and a cooler outer jacket into electricity, using a principle which was discovered almost 150 years ago. According to this principle, you can produce an electrical current by twisting two wires made of different metals into a loop and then heating one end of the loop. SNAP C-7 uses this old idea in a new way, with a modern heat source.

The electrical equipment for the weather station sits directly above SNAP 7-C, so there is no fear of the equip-

The SNAP 7-C atomic generator is lowered into a pit in the ice, where it now powers an automatic weather station.

ment's freezing. The measuring devices themselves are kept separate from the heat by insulation, but the whole automatic station fits inside a large metal container which is buried in the ice. Wooden outriggers keep it from sinking, and only a whip antenna projects above the surface. At least four times a day, the weather station goes on the air, transmitting information about temperature, wind direction, wind speed and barometric pressure.

According to the Antarctic Treaty, such peaceful uses of atomic energy are allowed as long as no radioactive waste is dumped on the continent. A generator like SNAP 7-C is so solidly built that its container would not split open even if a plane carrying it crashed and burned. It contains radioactivity, but it is so thoroughly sealed up that a man could sit right next to it indefinitely without being harmed.

Over the course of several years, however, the nuclear power plant at McMurdo Sound will produce some waste products which will have to be removed. They are not dangerous as long as they stay in the reactor tank, but there is no place to get rid of them — legally or practically — in Antarctica itself. From time to time the waste will be cleaned out and placed in sealed containers, then shipped all the way back to the United States for safe disposal. Some officials have called it "the longest garbage run in history."

To make sure that radioactive materials will not get into the Antarctic atmosphere accidentally, the three cylindrical tanks which contain the McMurdo reactor system are made of very heavy steel and reinforced by strong rings. They are also connected to an extra tank which is kept empty. Thus, in case the system "boils over," there is enough room for any gases which might result to expand safely without bursting the big metal containers.

Nuclear power has set the stage for broader, safer, and

more comfortable operations in the Antarctic. To some old-timers, however, it contributes something more — cleanliness. "When I first came here," said one veteran of the early expeditions, "Antarctica was the cleanest place in the world. But we had to bring fire with us, and that meant smoke and soot.

"Diesels were a big improvement so far as power goes, but they still covered the camps with black dust. I think morale will get a boost from the use of nuclear power. It produces no smoke, and this place is prettier without it."

CHAPTER TEN

Why Are We There?

Antarctica's most important export is scientific information. It comes in various shapes, from graph paper to fishheads to refrigerated metal cylinders full of ice. About 10 tons of records and specimens are produced annually by the U. S. teams alone; and many of their scientific projects have already been described in the preceding chapters.

Some of these studies are made because the Antarctic is exciting and different. We can never tell whether this kind of research will do us any practical good or not, because the scientists themselves don't know exactly what they will find. Occasionally they are not even sure of what to look for, or how to interpret the results when they get them. In other cases, Antarctic investigations are of immediate value. They supply important pieces which have been missing from our jigsaw-puzzle picture of the earth as a whole. One example of this is Antarctic meteorology.

Weather balloons are launched daily in Antarctica, even in the
dark of winter.

Twice a day at a typical Antarctic base, a helium-filled
balloon bobs up into the dazzling sunlight. The balloon's
fragile, dull white surface puckers in the wind; and for
a moment it looks as if it may turn inside out or go crashing into the ground. Then, finally, the balloon is caught
by an updraft and goes soaring aloft. Drifting lightly
upward to an altitude of 20 miles or more, its instrument
package will radio back the direction and speed of the
winds, the temperature and moisture content of the air.
In some parts of the continent measurements like these

A rocket zooms skyward to measure temperature and winds high above McMurdo Sound.

are made at ground level. At times, weather rockets have also been fired.

The Arcas rockets in these experiments are much smaller than the ones used by our space program; each one is only about eight feet tall and as big around as a rainspout. But their solid propellants can boost meteorological instruments 35 to 40 miles above the earth's surface, far beyond the reach of the balloons.

Scientists are interested in Antarctic weather because the southern continent helps to control the climate of the entire globe. If the earth didn't get rid of the heat it absorbs from the sun, it would get hotter and hotter until it melted. To keep our temperature at a reasonable level, the huge Antarctic region must do its share in radiating heat.

Surprisingly, Antarctica gets a bigger dose of the sun's energy than any other spot on earth. It tops the Arctic in this respect because the earth is closest to the sun during the Antarctic summer, when there is constant daylight at the South Pole. Of course, the sun's rays strike both of the earth's poles at a sharp angle — instead of head on, as they do at the equator. Thus they don't produce as much heat. Furthermore, solar heat bounces off the gleaming snow, just as light does. Only a tiny bit of the solar energy which strikes the Antarctic is retained.

This is one of the reasons why Antarctica is the world's icebox. There are other reasons, too. The presence of large bodies of open water tends to keep a place from getting too cold . . . but Antarctica is a desert, and much of the surrounding ocean is covered by ice for a good part of the year. Altitude is another factor . . . and Antarctica is the highest of all continents on earth. In the interior of the high polar plateau, temperatures of more than 125 degrees below zero have been recorded.

Antarctica manufactures more cold air than any other place in the world. The ice-crisp air rolls down the polar slope toward the coast, and the steepness of the coastal slope adds to its speed. When these winds reach a certain velocity, however, they seem to shift into high gear; they whirl along faster and faster. On the coast south of Australia, gusts sometimes reach 200 miles an hour.

Cold air from Antarctica mixes gradually with the warmer air to the north. Eventually, some of it may sweep across South Africa, Chile, Argentina and parts of Australia and New Zealand. As the population in these coun-

"Rotor clouds" are a sign of high winds over Antarctica, where much of the Southern Hemisphere's weather is born.

tries expands, it will become more and more desirable to understand the source of the chilling winds. Long-range weather prediction depends on it.

The Antarctic Ocean plays an even more direct role in controlling climate. The great southern ocean covers more than one-fifth of the earth's water surface, yet it contains only one-tenth of the seas' heat. Cold ocean currents can move northward more readily than the cold Antarctic air; and their effect is similar.

Shiploads of scientists are studying the way Antarctic waters circulate. They measure the currents, test their mineral content, and take their temperature at various levels. They bounce sound waves off the bottom to measure its depth, and they dredge up samples of the sediment from the ocean floor. Their findings are combined and compared with reports by the men studying Antarctic weather and Antarctic glaciers. Taken together, these bits of information will eventually draw a sharper picture of the whole southern hemisphere's climate.

Aside from weather, there are some aspects of nature which can be studied only in Antarctica. An example is the so-called "southern lights" which frequently break up radio communications. These shimmering displays of color in the sky — like those seen in the Far North — have been observed for centuries. Yet nobody can really explain them. There are theories, of course; and observations in Antarctica during the last 10 years or so are gradually building proof for some of these.

This much seems fairly certain: When pieces of matter shooting out from the sun strike our atmosphere, they upset the atoms of oxygen and nitrogen in the air. Each collision with these atoms jars loose some electrons — the tiny particles which normally whirl around the nucleus of each atom. Eventually the electrons and the short-changed atoms get together again, and, when they do, the energy which was stored up by the initial impact is released. The result is a little flash of light. Multiply this flash by 100,000 times per square inch and you get the fireworks called aurora australis — southern lights. (The same effect in the vicinity of the other pole is called aurora borealis — northern lights.)

If this theory is completely true, you may wonder why we don't normally see the lights over New York or Washington. The reason is that the earth acts like a gigantic magnet in space. If you hold a magnet under a piece of paper and sprinkle iron filings on the paper, the bits of iron will collect along a series of curves connecting the two poles of the magnet. These arcs are called "magnetic

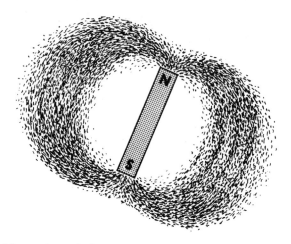

lines of force," and the earth has them, too. Solar particles collect along the arcs around the earth, just as the bits of iron do on the piece of paper. Near the ends of the globe, the lines of force swing down *through* the atmosphere and touch the earth. It is only here that the particles disturb the atmosphere and produce the color flashes. Thus artificial auroras can be produced by high-altitude nuclear explosions, which release charged particles in the very midst of the magnetic field.

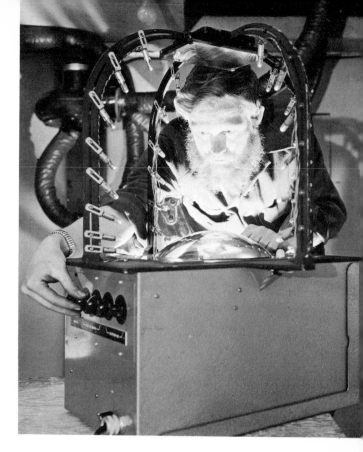

The Southern Lights are photographed by this all-sky camera, which uses a curved mirror to take a picture from horizon to horizon.

Incidentally, the spots at which the lines of magnetic force come to earth are called the geomagnetic poles. The one in Antarctica is on the polar plateau, about 800 miles away from the geographic pole. Its location has nothing at all to do with the South Magnetic Pole, which is the one we think of in connection with compasses.

The best place to study the southern lights, of course, is where you can see them best. This is in Antarctica. It also is useful to carry on studies of both the northern and southern lights at the same time, since we know now that these displays take place within an hour of each other at both ends of the earth. Ideally, observations should be made along the same line of force. Therefore, directly opposite Byrd Station is a scientific base at Great Whale River, Canada. Corresponding to Eights Station is another base in Quebec. And so on.

If auroral displays take place simultaneously in both hemispheres, some obviously go on in daylight. When it is summer daylight at the South Pole it is winter dark at the North Pole, and vice versa. The lights aren't usually bright enough to be visible in sunlight, though, so scientists watch them with radar.

Aurora glows are beautiful to see against a darkened sky. Most auroras are pale yellow-green, but they may also be red or bright blue. They often appear in arcs; but unlike rainbows they seem to cover the whole sky. The most active auroras give the impression of spotlighted drapes, being opened and closed slowly in the black heavens. Close to the geomagnetic pole itself, auroras have also been known to appear in double arcs, spilling across the sky in two directions at once to form a giant, eerie cross. It's no wonder that the first people to see the auroral lights were terrified. Many primitive people considered them a religious symbol of some kind.

The scientists who investigate auroras can also study other occurrences connected with the earth's magnetic field. Among these are "whistlers" — the strange radio signals which are produced by lightning. These signals start as ordinary static, but they are stretched out as they race along the lines of force. They produce a whistling sound in radio receivers, and this is where they got their nickname. Someday, scientists may be able to harness these signals and use them to study the fringes of space through which they pass. Antarctica is an especially fine place to study whistlers because it is so quiet. Lightning is rare, and there are few man-made electrical disturbances to clutter up the airwaves.

Radio noises in the upper
atmosphere are recorded and studied at Byrd Station.

If all this seems very high-flown, don't think that Antarctic research is never down to earth. In fact, one of the biggest areas of scientific study there is the earth itself — mapping the millions of landmarks in a vast, unpopulated land which generally has been seen only from the air.

Accurate maps are needed to make sense out of other scientific observations. A geologist likes to know precisely where his rock specimens come from. A glaciologist wants to be able to measure the full size and movement of Antarctica's giant ice rivers. In the long run, geography also contributes to the broadest of Antarctic operations. It

169

may help to decide where a new station should be established — or which ground routes should be used to get there.

Making maps is always tedious, but Antarctic terrain makes it even more difficult. Nevertheless, U.S. cartographers have now covered a huge slice of the continent, stretching from Hallett Station and the area northwest of McMurdo almost all the way to the geographic South Pole, then over toward the coast again in the direction of South America.

This region, nearly as big as our entire East Coast, is now mapped in more detail than some sections of the western United States.

A mapping team normally consists of three men, plus support groups to help them move around. Starting from a spot which is definitely located on existing charts, the party sends one man to a high point about 20 miles ahead. This distance may vary, because the lead man must make sure there is a clear line of sight between him and his companions when they are ready to make measurements. Once he is in place, he sets up two targets — a bright red framework of wood and cloth for rough sighting and a piece of electronic equipment which will capture and send back a signal from the master unit. The two-piece electronic instrument is called a Tellurometer, and it measures the time a signal takes to bounce back and forth, computing the distance within an accuracy of two inches over a span of 20 miles. Other instruments are used to check the angle — which determines the exact elevation and map location of the advance spot. Then a brass tablet with the correct altitude, latitude and longitude is hammered right into the rock. Sightings are made of other peaks to the right or left, and then the men are all set to move on. Using a helicopter, the rear party occupies the site of the new bench mark, and the lead

Antarctic map makers flash signals back and forth between two instruments like this to measure ground distances with great accuracy.

man is whisked 20 miles or so farther along the trail. Later, of course, these accurate positions will make it possible to interpret old and new aerial photographs.

Occasionally, scientists in Antarctica make a discovery which clearly may be of practical use to mankind. One example is the antibiotic discovered during the studies of penguins. A bacteriologist who had become interested in Antarctica was fascinated by the fact that penguins never seem to get upset stomachs. In fact, their digestive tracts are almost invariably free of disease. The scientist traced the cause of their good fortune to the penguins' diet. The birds eat a form of shrimp, which in turn eat

171

small green sea plants, which produce the antibiotic. Converted into medicine, the substance has proved effective against boils, abcesses and several other troublesome ailments.

Someday, perhaps, studies of the common cold in Antarctica will offer the same sort of dramatic results. Scientists don't expect to find a cold cure there, but they do consider it a superb place to carry on their studies. Groups of men who spend the winter in Antarctica are rarely bothered by colds during their isolation; but the first arrival of summer visitors soon has everybody sniffling again. The men of the wintering-over party thus become unintentional laboratory specimens for cold research.

The natural resistance of the human body is another logical thing to study in Antarctica. Skin divers who have gone under the ice near McMurdo Sound to study seals with cameras, lights and tape recorders have become an object of scientific study themselves. In physiological tests, a diver with an aqualung may stay motionless under water for almost half an hour while instruments record his heartbeat, breathing and temperature. The water temperature is higher than that of the air above, but a dip like this is still quite an ordeal. A man's skin temperature may drop 30 degrees, but it will gradually climb again as his body begins to adjust to the unfamiliar surroundings.

At inland bases, volunteers have braved temperatures down to more than 100 degrees below zero to let scientists study their reactions. One thing they have learned is that wind increases the chilling effect on the body. A 30-mile-an-hour wind in zero weather produces about the same effect as a temperature of -30 on a calm day. Someday these uncomfortable experiments may teach man to adjust himself more readily to bitter cold.

Scientists have also been curious about the reaction of plants and animals brought to the Antarctic. What happens to hamsters, fruit flies and certain plants, which seem to operate according to mysterious natural clocks? Somehow, nature has accustomed these creatures to operate on a daily schedule — a 24-hour schedule. Early studies had proved that their life cycles were not based entirely on periods of alternating light and darkness; but some biologists thought that the mysterious inner rhythm might have something to do with the earth's rotation. Experiments in Antarctica — where the earth's rotation is much less noticeable — proved that this guess was wrong. Despite the drastic change in environment, the biological clocks never missed a tick. Scientists in our space program, faced with the problem of sending men on long trips where day and night will be meaningless terms, are still looking for the right solution.

Generally speaking, most of the work in Antarctica is not aimed at answering specific practical questions. It is basic research. It is an effort to expand man's knowledge of the world in which he lives. Whether it contributes to his comfort and efficiency or not, new knowledge helps to raise man above the level of brute animals by sharpening his intellect and opening new horizons for his thought. It is with all these objectives in mind that the National Science Foundation sponsors its continuous Antarctic Research Program.

A scientist who wants to study some aspect of the Antarctic may write to or visit the National Science Foundation. He tells the Office of Antarctic Programs what he wants to do, why he thinks it is important scientifically, and what help his project will need from U.S. Support Forces. If his plan is approved, he will get free military transportation, equipment and a cash grant to cover salary, expenses and the costs of publishing his re-

Biologists fish through 10 feet of ice to learn more about Antarctic marine life.

search results. Each year, many such offers arrive from some of the finest scientists in the country. Other nations have similar programs.

Antarctica began its history with a period of heroic effort which we might call its Age of Discovery. Once man got his bearings and learned to survive there, he began to look around a bit more at the places and things he had found. That was the continent's Age of Exploration.

Today things have advanced even further. Modern transportation, peaceful atomic energy, and carefully organized scientific programs have made this the Age of Development.

It is a time of rapid progress. It is the time to get used to the fact that Antarctica is more than just a big chunk of ice which few people ever see. It is a period when newspapers, magazines, movies, lectures and books can show us a new picture of Antarctica. The fuzzy portrait of years ago becomes sharper as we look at the continent through the eyes of geologists and geographers, biologists and physicists, oceanographers and weather scientists.

But we have not yet considered the future of Antarctica. We can also look ahead to a time when Antarctica will seem closer as well as clearer, when basic research will blend into activities of immediate value. We might call that era Antarctica's Age of Promise.

CHAPTER ELEVEN

All Aboard for Antarctica –
A Look into the Future

How long will it be before the Winter Olympics are held at McMurdo Sound? The idea seems preposterous right now ... but who would have guessed 100 years ago that the newly acquired American territory of Alaska would ever become a state? Antarctica has changed drastically in the little more than 50 years since Amundsen reached the South Pole; and it is almost bound to see even greater advances in the next half century.

In a way, aviation has barely begun to touch the Antarctic. Only one commercial airliner has ever landed on the continent — a Pan American World Airways plane which was chartered to fly to McMurdo in 1957. But new air routes in the Southern Hemisphere will surely cross the Antarctic regions, just as flights between the United States and Europe now zip past the North Pole.

176

South America, Africa and Australia have little need for such air traffic just yet. Nevertheless, an increase in population, industry and commerce is due. The 1970's will probably see commercial jets whistling through the "international air space" above Antarctica, following the shortest route between Buenos Aires and Melbourne.

No airline is likely to schedule such flights on a year-round basis, however, until there are a few changes on the continent itself. For instance, some all-weather landing fields will undoubtedly be built. One may be at Marble Point; perhaps another will be in the oasis area near the Russians' Mirnyy Base. They will be costly, of course. But, after all, so was the Panama Canal.

Antarctica itself could easily become a tourist attraction. Its scenery is magnificent, and its dry cold would be popular with ski and toboggan enthusiasts. Above all, it would be "someplace new and different" to spend a vacation. When the Argentine government offered two Antarctic tourist cruises in 1958, there were hundreds more applications than they could handle. For each 10-day voyage, the passengers were issued special clothing. Apparently, the excursions were a huge success; and the Chilean government tried an Antarctic tourist trip also.

More recently, the French have considered sponsoring tourist flights to the McMurdo Sound area during the summer. These would be especially attractive because there is so much of historic and scientific interest to see there. The huts used by Scott and Shackleton are still standing, perfectly preserved by the Antarctic's unusual climate. Mount Erebus and the beautiful Beardmore Glacier are not far away; and New Zealand's Scott Base is within walking distance. A short helicopter hop could even take the visitors to a penguin rookery.

Where would the tourists stay? A lodge is the obvious answer, whether operated by a hotel chain, the airline or some governmental agency. Such an enterprise might have to be approved by representatives of the nations which signed the Antarctic Treaty, but there seems to be no reason why any of them should object. The idea certainly suits the announced goal of using the region for peaceful purposes.

Surface travel in Antarctica still has lots of room for improvement. It will continue to grow safer, faster and more comfortable. No vehicle used in the Antarctic snows so far has been able to adapt itself to both hard and soft surfaces, but lots of engineers are working on the problem. The Swedes have recently built a snow car which offers some improvement. It steers by moving its rear tracks instead of its front tracks, so that it moves like a ship with a rudder. Maybe this method is part of the answer. Another possibility is the much-publicized "hover craft." Flying platforms are still only experimental, but they have proved that they can skim safely across either land or water, riding a few inches above the surface on a cushion of air. Once such "ground-effect machines" are perfected, the consistency of the snow shouldn't make any difference at all to an Antarctic traverse party.

In the distant future, polar caravans will almost certainly use nuclear energy; but right now we can only guess at how this will be done. The United States and the Soviet Union have both made preliminary designs of nuclear reactors which would be small enough to be moved around on tractors, and engineers have suggested at least three ways in which they might be used to lick the motor fuel problem in a place like Antarctica:

   1) Some feel that such a reactor should propel the tractor on which it is mounted, and that sleds should be hitched along behind to form an atomic snow train.

Atomic power could
revolutionize surface travel in Antarctica.

2) Others suggest that each mobile reactor be used to power a chemical processing plant, which would use nitrogen from the air and water from the snow to manufacture synthetic gasoline right on the spot. This would provide every major route in the Antarctic with filling stations which would never run dry.

3) Still others believe that the reactor should just generate electricity, so that snow tractors of the future will be able to operate on batteries. Once a day, each vehicle would recharge itself, simply by hooking up to the reactor power plant.

Man will also find new ways of moving around in the

"Ground effect machines" could skim across rough Antarctic snow, open water or smooth ice as easily as this five-seat hovercraft speeds across a patchwork of ice floes during winter tests in the Baltic Sea.

waters of Antarctica. For example, scientists there have just begun to use a sub-ice chamber which can carry three men at a time to a point more than 20 feet below the surface. It is heated, of course, and equipped with powerful floodlights. The men inside it will be able to study the behavior of seals over long periods; and they may solve at last the mystery of how seals navigate in the dark waters and find their way to air holes in the ice above.

In future seasons, other manned capsules may reach the very bottom of the sea under the ice; and later models will crawl across the bottom, seeking out the weird fish and odd plants which thrive there. Nuclear submarines will help, too, probing far under the ice shelves. In the deepest parts of the Antarctic Ocean, men may finally locate the hiding places of the giant squid which sometimes do battle with the largest of whales. And scientists may even find the grotesque creatures which have given

180

This sub-ice observation chamber is the forerunner of vehicles which will explore the seas under Antarctica's ice shelves.

rise to the ancient but continuing stories of sea serpents.

Atomic icebreakers will make it possible to reach every section of the Antarctic coast; and convoys will be able to carry heavy supplies to some bases during most of the summer, instead of only a few months.

When docking in Antarctica, ships will find the job made easier by melting devices, which will keep the water in the vicinity of the ship circulating constantly. Equipment like this has already been tested in Antarctica with some success, but it is not yet in general use.

With more sea traffic, the number of ships on the lookout for icebergs in southern waters will probably be increased. The Antarctic Ocean has no patrol like the one which covers the North Atlantic; but eventually an elaborate system of spotting and charting Antarctic icebergs will probably have to be set up. The ships may even be aided by blimps. These big balloons can stay aloft for over a week, and they are much more rugged than they look. During World War II they proved that they could hunt submarines in the coldest, stormiest weather.

"What will the "cities" of Antarctica look like in the future? Probably not much different from the bases of today; which is another way of saying that there will always be several kinds. Permanent inland stations will probably be dug into the ice like the one at Byrd. They will have nuclear power plants, of course; and they may use heated, surface-level greenhouses to provide fresh fruit and vegetables. Small experiments with chemical gardening have already worked at many Antarctic bases; and it seems a shame to let 24-hour sunshine go to waste, especially when the sight of growing plants and the taste of fresh salad would be such a fine morale booster.

Smaller outposts will follow the pattern set by Eights Station. They will use prefabricated buildings which can be delivered by air and set up quickly, then moved whenever necessary. Of course this doesn't mean that they will look just like the "packing-crate houses" at Eights now. The prefabs of the future may be made of completely different materials — new plastics or perhaps even inflatable walls, which could simply be pumped up on the spot with an air compressor. This idea has been tried, and with stronger materials it may become popular.

Just as cities on other continents tend to be located along rivers, the new stations in Antarctica are likely to be situated along the mountain ranges which break up the polar landscape — the Horlicks, the Ellsworths and the Forrestal Mountains. This will be for the convenience of those studying rock and glacier formations. Except for some spots which have special scientific significance (like

Indoor gardening is just a hobby now; but in the future it may provide fresh food for Antarcticans.

the geographic and geomagnetic poles), the polar plateau itself is much more likely to be dotted with automatic nuclear-powered weather stations than with manned bases.

Along the coast, the next decade should see the first paved roads in Antarctica. As populations expand in. the bases built on bare ground (like McMurdo), summer mud will eventually become too much of a nuisance to bear. Streets will begin to look like real streets. The buildings will change also. They will use sturdier materials, and they will be much better insulated.

This Is Antarctica

The well-dressed Antarctic traveler of the future won't need bulky clothing. Trim, electrically heated coveralls will be powered by pocket-sized batteries to keep men warm without weighing them down. There will probably be heated helmets, too — making Antarcticans look a little like astronauts.

So far as equipment is concerned, the Antarctic residents of the future will look back on today's as primitive. For instance, there is no reason why two-way television shouldn't link Antarctica with the other continents. Actually, closed-circuit TV was used in the Antarctic as early as 1958, and random television signals have been picked up from as far away as London. But soon the worldwide satellite relay system will make possible clear and consistent reception from anywhere in the world.

What will the television cameras see in the Antarctica of tomorrow? Will they ever show more than a scientific laboratory and a playground for rich tourists? The answer can be an emphatic "Yes."

Some islands north of Antarctica contain semiprecious stones like amethyst, opal, jasper and agate. The gems have been found there in such big blocks that a single chunk was hard for a man to lift. Similar deposits probably exist on the continent itself — along with diamonds. There are hundreds of mineral ores as well, including gold, silver and a fairly high grade of manganese (a valuable material used in making certain kinds of steel). For the present, most of these natural resources in Antarctica are out of reach. The continent is a long distance from regular shipping lanes, and mining under the snow would be terribly expensive anyway. But this may not always be so. Oil derricks have been set up on the islands north of the Canadian mainland, where the weather can be just as bad as in some parts of Antarctica; and the hope of eventual profit may encourage similar experiments at the other

184

end of the world. If mining and drilling methods improve, and if we begin to run short of certain critical minerals, Antarctica may yet get its share of prospectors.

Some officials in Argentina view Antarctica in quite another role — as a giant refrigerator. They have made several tests to see whether beef and other foodstuffs could be stored there without spoiling. So far, the results are encouraging. The transportation to and from this natural deep freezer would cost money, to be sure; but if a country had very large stocks of surplus food to store, the plan might someday make economic sense.

It seems hard to imagine that a complete desert — the coldest, emptiest, windiest area on earth — could ever support activities like these. And yet we may live to see every one of the prospects described in this chapter become a reality. This is not science fiction. *This is Antarctica.*

All aboard for Antarctica!

Index

189

The author

JOSEPH M. DUKERT, a free-lance consultant in marketing and industrial communications, has been writing about science for more than fifteen years. He visited Antarctica for the Martin Company to develop ideas for a film about the first use of nuclear energy there, and that movie — *Power for Continent 7* — received the equivalent of an Academy Award as the best industrial sales film of the year.

As a member of the Antarctican Society and the American Polar Society, Mr. Dukert maintains frequent contact with the U. S. Antarctic Projects Office, the Navy's Operation Deep Freeze, and the National Science Foundation's Antarctic Research Program.

A *magna cum laude* alumnus of Notre Dame, Mr. Dukert pursued graduate studies in world politics at Georgetown, Johns Hopkins and the Hopkins School of Advanced International Studies in Bologna, Italy. During the Korean War he served with 13th Air Force Intelligence in the Far East.